GLOBETROTTER™

Safari Guide

KENYA

D0684401

Safari Guide

KENYA

Dave and Val Richards

CONTENTS

INTRODUCTION

K enya is a land of contrasts; its habitats vary from the snow-covered shoulders of Mount Kenya, montane forests, tropical rainforests, dry semidesert and savannahs, to the mangrove forests along the coast. Examples of all of these habitats are protected by National Parks and Reserves.

This variety of habitats and the wildlife they contain is unsurpassed anywhere else in Africa. In the northeast are the arid lands of Samburu, Buffalo Springs and Shaba reserves, where a visitor can see wildlife that is found nowhere else, such as the endangered Grevy's zebra, the long-necked gerenuk, beisa oryx, reticulated giraffe and some very special birds. In the southwest there is the world-famous Masai Mara National Reserve, well known for its abundance of wildlife (and where it is not at all unusual to be able to see and photograph all of the Big Five – black rhino, buffalo, elephant, leopard and lion – in a single morning) and where, between July and September, the famous wildebeest migration is to be found. In between these two extremes are the mountain national parks of Mount Kenya and the Aberdares, and the Great Rift Valley. Certainly no safari can be complete without a visit to Lake Nakuru National Park and its flamingos. To complete the variety, there are a number of marine national parks and reserves along the coast.

**Top Spots
to See Animals**

Masai Mara National Reserve: big cats and the famous wildebeest migration.
Buffalo Springs/Samburu National Reserves: gerenuk, beisa oryx, reticulated giraffe and leopard.
Lake Nakuru National Park: flamingos, rhinos and leopard.
Amboseli National Park: elephants and views of Kilimanjaro.

Opposite top: A lioness and her cubs in the Masai Mara National Reserve.
Opposite centre: A private vehicle on safari in Amboseli National Park, with Kilimanjaro in the distance.
Opposite bottom: The distinctive Vulturine Guineafowl occur in flocks in dry bush country.

Introduction

Where to Spot the Big Five

Lion: a nocturnal hunter, but the easiest cat to see in the Masai Mara during the day.

Leopard: shy and nocturnal, it can usually be seen in the Masai Mara, Samburu and Lake Nakuru reserves on early morning and late afternoon drives.

Elephant: seen in most wildlife areas (except Nairobi and Saiwa Swamp national parks); the best place is Amboseli, around swamps at midday.

Buffalo: the most dangerous of Africa's animals, it can best be seen in the Masai Mara National Reserve and the Aberdare National Park.

Rhino: both black and white species are mostly confined to protected areas; see them in Nairobi, Nakuru and Aberdare national parks; Solio Ranch and Lewa Conservancy.

Kenya's national parks were founded in 1946. They offer the visitor a chance to experience and observe wildlife in its natural state in stunning scenic backgrounds. The wildlife that a visitor will see in the national parks and reserves has become so accustomed to safari vehicles, and their often noisy occupants, that the animals no longer run and hide, but carry on with their normal life. Prides of lions will often continue sleeping, which can at times be a little annoying for the visitor wanting to photograph a fierce lion! One thing is for sure, anyone visiting Kenya will never forget their amazing experiences and many visitors will return again and again.

It can be said that safaris started in Kenya. The word safari simply means 'a journey' in Kiswahili. In 1909 President Roosevelt set out from Nairobi's famed Norfolk Hotel on his famous year-long safari with two white hunters, JR Cuningham and William Judd, 15 askaris (soldiers) and 265 porters. Porters were paid $US4.50 per day, a licence to shoot an elephant was US$85.00, and for a rhino or a hippo it was US$15.00. On this safari Roosevelt and his son Kermit collected 1100 specimens, which included 17 lion, 11 elephant and 20 black rhino. The oldest operating safari company in Africa, Ker & Downey Safaris, based in Nairobi, celebrated its 60th birthday in 2006.

Safaris are a very important source of income for Kenya, being second only to agriculture in revenue earnings. So by visiting Kenya you are helping the economy and all of Kenya's people.

So Karibu (welcome), and enjoy your safari in Kenya.

PART ONE: PLANNING YOUR TRIP

When booking your safari it is very important to book with a reputable company, preferably a member of KATO (Kenya Association of Tour Operators). Ensure that your driver/guide is at least a Bronze level member of the KPSGA (Kenya Professional Safari Guides Association) and your tour leader is at least a Silver level member of the KPSGA. Pick an itinerary that stays at a destination for two or (even better) three nights. There is nothing more exhausting than to keep moving on every night, with long drives between destinations.

Part One: Planning your trip

Types of safari – special safaris

While most visitors take a general wildlife safari, you can book a safari specializing in a particular subject.

Balloon safaris

Balloon flights are available in the Masai Mara and in the Rift Valley, and can be arranged with your tour operator or from your camp or lodge. They take place at dawn which means an early wake-up as you have to drive to the launch site. In the Masai Mara there are a number of balloon companies.

Governors' Camp Balloons: based at Little Governors' Camp, www.governorscamp.com

Mara Balloons: based at Keekorok Lodge, Mara Safari Club, Mara Serena Lodge.

Trans World Safaris: tours@transworldsafaris.com

There are also balloon flights available over the Rift Valley. Guests are picked up from their lodge or camp at Lake Naivasha or Lake Nakuru. **Go Ballooning Kenya:** www.goballooningkenya.com

Bird shooting safaris

The shooting season for sandgrouse, guineafowl, francolin and spurfowl is 1 July to 31 October. The season for doves and pigeons is 1 June to 31 March. Operators include:

Ker & Downey Safaris: www.kerdowneysafaris.com

Above: A family of cheetahs sitting on a tourist vehicle, a not unusual sight in the Masai Mara National Reserve.

Introduction

Robin Hurt Safaris: www.robinhurtphotosafaris.com
Kulalu Camp, Galana Ranch: nick@swiftmalindi.com
Kalacha Camp, Chalbi Desert: www.tropicair-kenya.com
David Mead: www.kerdowneysafaris.com

Top Spots to See Birds

Kakamega Forest, Buffalo Springs/Samburu national parks (mountain), Mida Creek (coast), Arabuko-Sokoke Forest Reserve (coast).

Bird-watching safaris

With 1092 species recorded, Kenya is a prime birding destination. On a two-week safari as many as 500 species can be seen, while on a three-week safari during October through to March, when many Eurasian migrants visit, seeing 700 species is a distinct possibility.
Bird Ventures (Origins Safaris): www.originsafaris.info
Ben's Ecological Safaris: www.tcfb.com/bestours

Camel safaris

Camel safaris take place in northern Kenya where the camel is most suited. Safaris last from a few days to a week. Sleeping on a camp bed (covered with a net) under the stars is an unforgettable experience. Although visitors can ride a camel if they wish, the real wonder of this type of safaris is walking. On these safaris visitors are escorted by colourful Samburu tribesmen.
African Frontiers: www.geocities.com/african_frontiers
Sabuk Camel Safaris: www.eco-resorts.com/SabukCamels.php
Bobong and Ol Maisor Camels: olmaisor@africaonline.co.ke

Kenya's Ornithological Heritage

Kenya has 1092 bird species. In Africa only Zaire – four times larger in area than Kenya – has more species. Kenya holds the record for the largest number of birds seen in a 24-hour period: 340, seen by Terry Stevenson, John Fanshaw and Andy Roberts (a team from the USA has recorded a higher total in South America, but a substantial number of the birds were only heard and not seen). Kenya also holds the world record for the greatest number of birds seen in a 48-hour period: 496, seen by Don Turner, David Pearson and the world-famous wildlife film-maker, Alan Root.

Climbing safaris

To climb Africa's second highest mountain, Mount Kenya, is the ambition of climbers worldwide. A climb to the twin peaks, Batian (5199m/17,058ft) and Nelion (5188m/17,022ft), requires serious ice-climbing experience, but for lesser skilled climbers and walkers, Point Lenana (4985m/16,355ft), higher than Mont Blanc, is a good alternative. There are three climbing routes: the Naro-Moru Route, Sirimon Track and Chogoria Route. There is also an interesting Summit Circuit that circles the mountain.
Naro Moru Lodge: www.alliancehotels.com
Mountain Club of Kenya: www.mck.or.ke
Tropical Ice Safaris: www.tropical-ice.com

Cultural safaris

Most safari camps and lodges offer visits to local villages. In the northern districts its possible to visit isolated tribes in the Lake

Part One: Planning your trip

Turkana area, which is often described as the 'Cradle of Mankind.'
Origins Safaris: www.originsafaris.info/cradle-of-mankind.htm

Elephant safaris

In the Samburu National Reserve it is possible to join elephant researchers while they study the local elephant, and in Nairobi it is possible to visit Daphne Sheldrick's elephant orphanage.
Elephant Watch Safaris: www.elephantwatchsafaris.com
Sheldrick Animal Orphanage:
www.sheldrickwildlifetrust.org

Fishing safaris

Kenya has a lot to offer, from trout fishing in streams and mountain tarns on the Aberdares and Mount Kenya, and Lake Turkana in the hot far north, where you can fish for tiger fish, giant Nile perch, barbel and tilapia, to excellent sport fishing in the Indian Ocean. Guests staying at Mfangano Lodge and Rusinga Lodge, on Lake Victoria, can fish for Nile perch and tilapia. Sea fishing is on offer at most of the coastal hotels.
Brookside Fishing Flies Company:
www.flyfishingkenya.com
Ker & Downey Safaris: www.kerdowneysafaris.com
Hemingways Resort, Watamu: www.big-gamefishing.net
Sea Adventures Ltd., Shimoni: hemphill@biggame.com
Peponi Hotel, Lamu: www.peponi-lamu.com
Kingfisher Boats, Malindi: www.kenyasportsfishing.com
Howard Laurence-Brown, Mtwapa:
www.kenyadeepseafishing.net

Flying safaris

With over 400 airstrips in the country, an excellent domestic schedule, and charter airlines available, flying is becoming more and more popular. Domestic flights with Air Kenya and Safarilink from Nairobi's Wilson Airport fly to all the major safari destinations, while the charter airlines will fly you virtually anywhere.
Schedule Airlines
Air Kenya: www.airkenya.com
Safarilink: www.safarilink.co.ke
Air Charter Services
Boskovic Air Charters: www.boskovicaircharters.com

Scenic Beauty Spot

Great Rift Valley: there are stunning views looking down into the Great Rift Valley from near Nairobi and Maralal.

Best Times to Visit Kenya

It's possible to enjoy a safari all year round – even in the rainy season it rarely rains for more than a few hours each day and then usually only in the evenings. The most popular time for safaris is July to September. This is the time when the famous 'migration' takes place in the Masai Mara and when most schools in Europe and the USA are closed for the summer holidays.

Introduction

East African Air Charters: www.eaaircharters.co.ke
Everett Aviation (helicopter charters):
www.everettaviation.com
Tropic Air (based out of Nanyuki): www.tropicair-kenya.com
Naivasha Aviation Services (based out of Gilgil):
www.simpsonsafaris.com

Getting married

For some time now, it has been popular to get married while on holiday. More and more safari camps and lodges now offer this service too. At Governors' Camp in the Masai Mara, as well as regular marriage ceremonies, they can also arrange for couples to get married in a Masai *manyatta* by a Masai *labon* (holy man). This kind of marriage is not legal back home, of course. Information and photography: www.lynseyphotos.com

Golfing safaris

Few countries can offer golfing holidays that include wonderful wildlife and beautiful beaches. At some of the golf courses you may even have to wait for a hippo or a group of warthogs to move before you can tee off! There are 40 golf courses in Kenya, ten of which are used for championship events. Many of the

Below: Governors' Il Moran Camp on the banks of the Mara River in the Masai Mara National Reserve.

Part One: Planning your trip

courses are at an altitude of more than 1500m (5000ft) and are ideal for golfing all year round.

Kenya Golf Safaris: www.kenya-golf-safaris.com

Leisure Golf Club: www.golfinginkenya.com

Helicopter safaris

Tropic Air, based in Laikipia, offer visitors the unprecedented opportunity to discover and explore northern Kenya's remote and stunning areas with the ultimate in speed and comfort. Their Eurocopter is equipped with fly-fishing rods, so it's possible to fly to remote tarns and streams on Mount Kenya and fish for trout.

Tropic Air: www.tropicair-kenya.com

Horseback safaris

Several companies offer safaris by horseback. Itineraries include the Masai Mara, Amboseli, Chulu Hills and the stunning scenery of the Great Rift Valley. A new circuit takes in Meru and Laikipia and finishes in the Masai Mara. On these safaris your accommodation is in mobile camps that are set up for you each evening. It is also possible to take horse rides while staying at various safari lodges, such as Borana Lodge and Wilderness Trails Lewa Downs.

OffBeat Safaris: www.offbeatsafaris.com

Safaris Unlimited: www.safarisunlimited.com

The Safaricom Marathon

Runners from all over the world come to Lewa Downs to compete in the Safaricom Marathon. This is the only marathon in the world where runners run through a wildlife reserve. Although predominantly a fund-raising event, many professional runners also take part. The funds raised are used for education, health care and wildlife conservation in the area.

Safaricom Marathon: www.lewa.org/lewa_marathon.php

Railway safaris

East African Steam Safaris run two-day rail trips from Nairobi to Mombasa. A refurbished Beyer Garratt is used to pull the train. Stops are made at various vantage points for photography and for a candlelight dinner.

East African Steam Safaris: tannereps@iconnect.co.ke

Essentials for Your Medical Kit

Anti-malarial drugs

Aspirin (or similar)

Antihistamine (for insect bites and allergies)

Oral rehydration powder

Insect repellent

Lip balm

Alcoholic swabs

Scissors

Tweezers

Plasters (Band-Aids)

Anti-diarrhoea pills and laxatives (consult your pharmacist for advice)

Throat lozenges

Antiseptic cream

Insect bite cream

Eye drops

Any other medicines and toiletries you regularly use

Energy bar/drink for walking safari

Introduction

Klaas's Cuckoo was named by Francois Le Vaillant, a French naturalist and traveller who explored the Cape Province in 1781. The cuckoo was named after his Khoi Khoi servant, thought to have shown him the bird.

Verreaux's Eagle is named after a French naturalist and explorer, Jean Baptiste Edouard Verreaux. Together with his brother Jules, he worked in the Cape Colony sending stuffed birds to their family in Paris. They became notorious for 'preserving' the body of an African chief, which was on display in Barcelona until the late 20th century, when the chief's descendents demanded its return for a proper burial.

Wahlberg's Eagle is named after a Swedish naturalist and collector, John August Wahlberg, who travelled widely in southern Africa between 1838 and 1856. He sent thousands of specimens to Sweden and was eventually killed by an elephant.

Photographic safaris

It is possible to book a special photographic safari with most safari companies. Origins Safaris are the most experienced company in this field.

Origins Safaris: www.originsafaris.info
For Wildlife Filming, contact: samuels@swiftkenya.com

Scuba diving

Dogs Breath Divers: www.dogsbreathdivers.com/kenya
Ocean Sports: www.oceansports.net

Volunteer holidays

Join researchers as they radio track animals and monitor the behaviour of various species at the Taita Discovery Centre.
Origins Safaris: www.originsafaris.info

Sites of historical or cultural interest

Fort Jesus, Mombasa

This 16th-century stronghold was built by the Portuguese to protect their trade routes to India. The architect was Italian, so the structure has similar features to an Italian fortress of the time. The fort, whose walls are 15m (50ft) high and 2.4m (8ft) thick, stands on an old coral ridge at the entrance to the Old Harbour, Mombasa.

At the end of the 17th century, the Sultan of Oman sent an army to seize the fort; the siege lasted almost three years before it finally fell into their hands. In 1728 the fort was recovered by the Portuguese without a struggle, but relinquished again later to remain under Arab rule until 1895, when Mombasa became a British protectorate. The fort was bombarded by the British Navy in 1878 and 1895, when it became a prison under British protection. On 15 August 1960, Fort Jesus was declared a national monument.

Gedi Ruins

Sixteen kilometres (10 miles) south of Malindi, the ruins of an old Arab town, set in the midst of the coastal forest, provide an atmospheric reminder of the past. Gedi was founded in the 14th century and flourished during the late 14th and 15th centuries. It was abandoned in the early 17th century, probably because of

Part One: Planning your trip

increased pressure from the warlike Galla tribe as they moved southwards. The word 'Gedi', or, more correctly, 'Gede', is a Galla word meaning 'precious'; it is also a personal name. Gedi was originally surrounded by a 2.7m-high (9ft) wall, which has at least three gates. The northwestern part of the town has been excavated and covers an area of about 18ha (44 acres).

Among the excavated ruins are the Great Mosque (originally constructed in the 15th century and rebuilt 100 years later), the Palace, the Dated Tomb – inscribed with its Arabic date AH802 (1399) – and the Pillar Tomb. A number of wells are now the home of barn owls.

Interesting birds can be seen at Gedi, among them the Lizard Buzzard, Palm-nut Vulture, Trumpeter Hornbill, Narina Trogon and Black-breasted Glossy Starling. Blue monkeys and red-tailed squirrels also live among the ruins. Gedi is administered by the National Museums of Kenya and is open to the public daily from 07:00 to 18:00.

Below: The ruins of Gedi, an old Arab town founded in the 14th century. Gedi flourished in the 14th and 15th centuries, but was mysteriously abandoned in the early 17th century.

Vasco da Gama Pillar
At Malindi, Vasco da Gama cross and church, built in 1541, are open to the public. Sheik Hassan's pillar tomb, standing beside a 19th-century pillar tomb, can also be seen on the waterfront next to the mosque.

Jumba la Mwtana
The Slave Master's House north of Mtwapa Creek is a monument that forms part of an ancient city that was abandoned some time between the 14th and 15th centuries. The atmospheric ruins, which have been declared a national monument, are set at the edge of the beach among baobab trees and consist of four mosques (one of which is gently subsiding into the sands), some houses and a cemetery.

Aberdare National Park
This was the hideout of the legendary freedom fighter, 'Field Marshall Kimathi'.

Introduction

* 1–2 pairs of smart/casual trousers
* 3–4 pairs of shorts
* 7 shirts/T-shirts (any combination)
* A light cotton dress/sarong for the ladies
* A lightweight fleece or sweater for the evenings
* A tracksuit
* A windbreaker/rain jacket
* A warm jacket
* A pair of walking/running shoes
* A pair of sandals/thongs
* Underwear and socks
* Swimming costume
* Wide-brimmed sun hat
* Towel

Treetops

The site where Princess Elizabeth became Queen in 1952.

Kenyatta House, Maralal

The house where Kenya's first president, Jomo Kenyatta, was detained prior to his final release in 1961.

Accommodation

A wide range of accommodation is available for travellers going on safari in Kenya, ranging from simple bungalows, small camps, mobile safaris and large tented camps to home-stays and luxury Safari lodges with private suites. Almost the only self-catering accommodation available on safari are those establishments run by the Kenya Wildlife Service, e-mail: tourism@kws.org website: www.kws.org

There is a star system of grading accommodation in Kenya, but unfortunately it is based on a system where a large safari lodge of over 100 rooms will have a high number of stars than a smaller one, simply because it has more than one restaurant or because it has a games room. The smaller permanent tented camps, such as Il Moran Camp in the Masai Mara National Reserve, are often far superior to any safari lodge, but with only 10 tents, it has a rating of only a few stars because it does not have a swimming pool and has only one restaurant!

The type of accommodation you choose can make a big difference to your safari experience. In general, guests receive more personal attention at the smaller tented camps, while the large lodges are far less flexible and tend to stick to more strict schedules – although they do tend to have better food and service. The smaller camps, in particular the mobile camping safaris, will amend their schedules to suit their guests.

Almost all of the large safari lodges and camps have swimming pools, TV rooms and massage rooms, and most are surrounded by electric fences so that the guests do not have to fear encountering an elephant or hippo. But to experience the real Africa it is far better for visitors to stay in the smaller tented camps that have no fences, where they have a good chance of

Part One: Planning your trip

hearing the sounds of the wild while lying in their tent. All in all, staying in a camp is a far better safari experience.

It is also possible to stay at ranches that have wildlife on their land, Loisaba being a good example. Private homes are also available, particularly around Lake Naivasha. The Kenya Wildlife Service has self-catering cottages and houses available in some of the national parks. For information, contact the Kenya Wildlife Service on e-mail: tourism@kws.org or visit their website at www.kws.org

What to pack

Space in the safari vehicle and in small aircraft is limited, so your luggage should be restricted to:

• A bag, preferably a soft one, not exceeding 12kg (26lb) in weight and 65x46cm (25x18in) in dimension.
• A small handbag (airline type) or daypack for money, travel documents and camera equipment.
• A waist pouch or money belt.
• A small fold-up bag to be used on itineraries that include optional short excursions.

Clothing and personal effects

Most people make the mistake of taking too much clothing. Bring comfortable wash-and-wear clothes, both casual and semi-casual. Bright colours and white are not suitable for game-viewing. Please avoid clothing resembling an army uniform (i.e. camouflage clothing). The list of clothing in the panel on page 16 is just a guideline and will depend on the duration of the safari as well as the season in which you are travelling – additional warmer clothing may be required during the rainy seasons (the long rains are in March–June, short rains October–November).

If, during your safari, you are visiting Lamu or Zanzibar, as a form of respect to local customs and the Islamic religion, ladies are requested to dress discreetly by covering their knees and shoulders.

Also remember to pack the personal effects recommended in the panel on this page.

What to Pack – Personal Effects

• Insect repellent
• A good pair of lightweight binoculars for each person
• Sunglasses
• Sunscreen
• Torch (flashlight)
• Medical kit (see panel, page 13)
• One-litre water bottle per person (essential)
• One torch and batteries per person (essential)
• Toilet paper
• Bath soap
• Toothbrush and toothpaste
• Shampoo and hair conditioner
• Deodorant
• Comb/hair brush, nail brush
• Razor and blades
• Lip balm
• Hand cream and moisturizing cream
• Tissues or disposable moist tissues
• Plastic bag (to pack wet/dirty clothing)
• Spectacles (if worn) – some people have trouble with contact lenses and dust
• Pen for immigration formalities
• Note book
• Multipurpose knife (e.g. Swiss Army Knife)

Introduction

Habitats and Biomes

Kenya's landscape is characterized by its huge diversity. Almost every known type of landform, from snow-covered mountains and glaciers to desert, occurs within its boundaries, also freshwater lakes Baringo, Naivasha and Lake Victoria, and soda (alkaline) lakes such as lakes Bogoria, Elementaita, Magadi and Nakuru. The land has some of Africa's oldest eroded plains and also some of its youngest, created by recent volcanic activity. Biomes include deserts and semi-deserts, grassland, coastal forest, rainforest, montane forest, ground water forest, highlands, moorland, savannah, mangrove, acacia savannah and acacia woodland.

PART TWO: ECO ISSUES AND CLIMATE

Kenya's safari code

Keep to designated roads or tracks. Encourage your driver/guide to stay on roads or designated tracks when visiting national parks and reserves. Off-road driving can cause extensive damage to grass and woodland habitats.

Minimize disturbance to animals. Wild animals become distressed when they are surrounded by several vehicles or when vehicles come too close to them. Keep noise to a minimum and never try to attract an animal's attention.

Stay inside your vehicle at all times. Do not stand on the roof or hang out of the windows, and only leave your vehicle at designated areas. Remember, wild animals can be dangerous.

Keep to the speed limit. Most wildlife areas have a speed limit of 40kph (25mph), and animals have right of way – always.

Right: An unusual road sign, erected in an effort to stop colobus monkeys from being run over by speeding vehicles.

Part Two: Eco issues and climate

Support eco-friendly accommodation facilities. Try to stay in lodges and camps that look after their environment and support local conservation initiatives.

Never feed any animals. Feeding wild animals can upset their diet and lead to an unnatural dependence upon people.

Take care not to disturb the ecological balance. Do not purchase, collect or remove any animal products, rocks, seeds or bird's nests from the wild or alter the natural environment in any way.

Take your litter with you. Litter and garbage are dangerous to wild animals. Keep all litter with you and be very careful with cigarettes and matches, which can cause major bush fires.

The protection of Kenya's natural environment is a responsibility that is shared by the tourist industry, the local people and also visitors. As a visitor to Kenya you have the power to influence the behaviour of others. If you see an incident that clearly contravenes any of the above guidelines, please record this and request an incident report form from the reception of your hotel or lodge. If you insist that these guidelines are adhered to, you will be playing an important part in helping Kenya to preserve some of the world's greatest wilderness areas.

Climate

Although Kenya straddles the equator, much of the country is not tropical. Because of the huge variation in altitude there are extensive differences in temperatures; a large amount of the land has an altitude of over 1200m (4000ft) and during the rains may be quite cool for extended periods. Above 2400m (8000ft) it can be cold, with snow falling on the higher slopes of Mount Kenya and sleet and hail falling on the highlands, including the Nairobi area at 1650m (5400ft). The coastal strip and Lake Victoria area are warm to hot with high humidity, while the northeastern and eastern lowlands are hot and mostly dry.

Kenya is influenced by two air masses at different times of the year. A northeasterly air mass originating in Arabia and the Horn

Mammals Named After People

Thomson's gazelle was named by Joseph Thomson, an English explorer who explored what is now Kenya in the late 1800s. He wrote a book, *Walk Through Masai Land*, about his travels.

Grant's gazelle was named after James Grant, a British explorer.

Burchell's (common) zebra was named after William John Burchell, an English explorer and collector who explored the interior of Southern Africa between 1811 and 1815 and walked more than 7000km (4350 miles). Burchell was the first European to describe a white rhino.

Introduction

Environmental Organizations

The Kenya Wildlife Service (KWS) is charged with the protection and conservation of the country's biodiversity – its fauna and flora.
Website: www.kws.org

The Ecotourism Society of Kenya is dedicated to creating an awareness of ecotourism through mobilization and education of local people and tour operators.
Website: www.esok.org

The East African Wildlife Society produces a great wildlife magazine.
Website: www.eawildlife.org

Nature Kenya has many different projects, connecting nature and people.
Website: www.naturekenya.org

of Africa dominates from November to March, usually bringing hot and dry weather. From April to July a warm, humid air mass brings rain in from the Indian Ocean. It is these air masses that have been used for centuries by Arab and Chinese traders to sail to and from East Africa. Another moist, westerly air mass, originating over the Atlantic Ocean and the Zaire Basin, brings rain to western Kenya, mainly in August.

Rainfall varies greatly – in quantity as well as seasonally. Most of the north and northeast receives as little as 255mm (10in) of rainfall annually, while Mount Kenya and western Kenya average 2000mm (80in), and most highland forests (Aberdares) receive over 1000mm (40in) annually. The costal strip receives over 800mm (32in), but this often rises to 1200mm (42in) between April and July, with May being the wettest month. The Masai Mara National Reserve, which is influenced by the weather of the Lake Victoria area, receives over 1000mm (40in) of rain, mostly from December to May, but it can receive rain showers in almost any month. The area east of the Rift Valley experiences two distinct annual rainy seasons – the 'long rains', between March and May, and the 'short rains', from November to December. These rains are not always predictable. Some years the rains are late or fail completely.

The world's greatest wildlife spectacle

The annual migration of wildebeest and other animals in the Serengeti and Masai Mara is well known. During the course of a year the wildebeest make a trek of anything from 800–1600km (500–1000 miles) as they circle the ecosystem. Their actual route varies from year to year and depends on rainfall that produces the grass on which the wildebeest herds feed. You often read about – or see on television wildlife programs – people talking of the start and finish of the migration. There is no start or finish as such; the migration is a continual movement of the herds in search of food and water. If there is a time that you could call the start of the migration, it is birth. All births take place in the short grass plains in the southeastern part of the Serengeti ecosystem. These plains consist of fine volcanic soils that have been blown there from the Crater Highlands (Ngorongoro crater is one) over millions of years. These soils are rich in minerals, calcium and phosphorus, but for most of the year they are desolate,

Part Two: Eco issues and climate

providing little food and no water for the few Grant's gazelle and ostrich that somehow survive here.

By January or February the rains arrive and the area turns green almost overnight, providing the wildebeest with mineral-rich grazing. These open plains have another advantage for the wildebeest: it is very difficult for any predator to approach the herds without being seen. Within days the female wildebeest herd together and start giving birth; 80% of the females will give birth within a few weeks. This glut of births is thought to be an anti-predator behaviour – with so many calves, it decreases the chances of a calf being singled out by a predator. The predators also become glutted by the sheer numbers of calves available, so more calves will survive the first crucial weeks.

By March/April these open plains start to dry out, forcing the wildebeest to move on. Usually they move in a northwesterly direction towards an area known as the Western Corridor and Lake Victoria, which consists of open woodlands. It is in this area during May to June that the rut (mating season) takes place. By the end of June the grazing begins to get sparse and the herds slowly head northwards towards the Masai Mara National Reserve, the first ones usually arriving during early July. There is a popular misconception that the herds have to cross the Mara River to arrive in Kenya and the Masai Mara National Reserve.

Plants of Special Interest

Mountain national parks: alpine heath zone, groundsels (senecios), and giant lobelia.

Shimba Hills National Reserve: some rare cycads and a small primitive palm.

Below: Landscapes of Kenya – the dramatic Rift Valley view from near Nairobi (left), and a lion in the dry grasslands of the Masai Mara (right).

Introduction

Topography

Kenya has a distinctive topographic profile. The interior is much higher than the rest of the country, and the mountains are roughly in a line running north and south. Its highest mountain, Mount Kenya, is located in approximately the centre of the country. The Great Rift Valley runs from north to south through Kenya, separating the Lake Victoria basin to the west from the hills in the east, which slowly descend into the dry grassy lowlands and coastal beaches. Kenya's topography forms complex ecological zones, including one called the highland zone. This is a region of rolling uplands characterized by cool weather, abundant rainfall, rich volcanic soils, and dense human settlement.

The border between Kenya and Tanzania is a line on the map – not the Mara River. Of course, during the herds' time in the Masai Mara they do cross the Mara River several times as they seek good grazing. When the herds arrive at the Mara River they often stand for hours before they decide to cross, and frequently change their minds at the last minute. Very often the herds of zebra that accompany the wildebeest on their migration make the first move and the wildebeest follow them across the river. Because of this behaviour the wildebeest are thought by some to be stupid, but Dr Richard Estes, who has studied wildebeest for over 30 years, has a theory. The zebra herds are made up of family groups – a stallion and three or four mares and their foals. These family units know each other well and inspire the confidence to decide to cross the Mara River. By comparison,

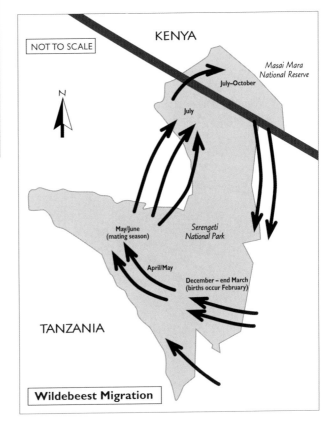

NOT TO SCALE

KENYA

Masai Mara
National Reserve

July–October

N

July

May/June
(mating season)

Serengeti
National Park

April/May

December – end March
(births occur February)

TANZANIA

Wildebeest Migration

Part Two: Eco issues and climate

wildebeest do not have family groups; the only stable association a wildebeest has is between mother and calf. In effect, therefore, a herd of wildebeest deciding to cross the river are almost all strangers to one another.

These crossings can be spectacular to watch and it can be unbelievable at times to see the wildebeest jumping down the river banks, which can be 5–6m (16–20ft) high, without apparently hurting themselves. Once in the river they often have to face some of the largest crocodiles in Africa, but most make it safely across. Problems arise when the river bank they are climbing up gets wet and slippery as more and more wildebeest try to climb out of the river. Many just cannot make it up the steep, slippery banks and fall exhausted down into the river where they drown.

Above: Wildebeest crossing the Mara River in the Masai Mara National Reserve.

During these crossings many calves get separated from their mothers and females can be seen swimming back and forth across the river calling their calves. After a major crossing there are always a few females and calves running back and forth parallel to the herd calling for each other, and it is common to see numbers of sad-looking calves grouped together, not knowing which way to turn. Even though the calves would be eating grass, the chances of them surviving without the protection of their mothers are thought to be slim – no one knows for certain how many do eventually perish without their mothers' protection. The herds usually stay in the Masai Mara until late September, before again heading southwards towards the short grass plains of the Serengeti where the whole drama will begin again. The actual departure date can never be accurately predicted, as again it all depends on the amount of grass available in the Masai Mara and when grazing becomes available in the Serengeti.

NAIROBI, OL-DOINYO SABUK AND AMBOSELI

This chapter covers three very different national parks. Amboseli is perhaps Kenya's best-known wildlife area, while Ol-Doinyo Sabuk is almost certainly one of the least known. Both of these parks are very different to Nairobi National Park, which is the only wildlife refuge in the world situated close to a major city. Amboseli has a Hollywood image: the magnificent backdrop of Africa's highest mountain, with herds of zebra, elephant and wildebeest feeding in the foreground, has been used by film-makers many times. But no matter how many times you have seen Kilimanjaro in films or magazines, nothing can prepare you for your first breathtaking view of this magnificent mountain/volcano. By contrast, the background to Nairobi National Park is the skyline of a major city. At Ol-Doinyo Sabuk, a mountain is the national park and the views, although invigorating, are of farms and plains with the city of Nairobi in the distance. On clear days Kilimanjaro and Mount Kenya can also be seen from here.

Top Ten

Elephants (including some males with big tusks)
Fringe-eared oryx
Lion
Cheetah
Yellow baboon
Saddle-billed Stork
Long-toed Plover (Lapwing)
Double-banded Courser
African Fish Eagle
Pink-backed Pelican

Opposite, top to bottom: A herd of elephants in Amboseli National Park; the bar and dining area at Tortilis Camp, Amboseli; a herd of common (Burchell's) zebra feeding in Amboseli National Park.

Nairobi National Park

Nairobi National Park

Location: 8km (5 miles) from central Nairobi.

Size: 120km² (46 sq miles).

Altitude: 1533–1760m (5030–5775ft).

Of interest: Nairobi is the only city in Africa where one can get into a car outside your hotel and be in wild Africa in 20 minutes (traffic allowing).

Accommodation:

Holiday Inn: www.southernsun.com

Jacaranda Hotel: www.jacarandahotels.com

Hotel La Mada and Oakwood Hotel: www.madahotels.com

Palacina Hotel: www.palacina.com

Fairview Hotel: www.fairviewkenya.com

Norfolk Hotel: www.lonrhohotels.com

Nairobi National Park was Kenya's first national park and it owes its existence to one man, the late Mervyn Cowie. Mervyn had tried for years to get the British government to create the national park and in desperation wrote a letter to the local newspaper calling for all the wildlife in the area to be destroyed as the wildlife was destroying the grazing used by cattle and goats. He signed the letter 'Old Settler'. This created such an uproar that a committee was formed and at the end of World War II (1946) the area was gazetted a national park. Mervyn was its first executive officer.

This unique area is only 8km (5 miles) from the city centre, and at only 120km² (46 sq miles) is entirely within the city's limits. It is the home of an amazing variety of wildlife – 80 mammal species and over 500 bird species have been recorded here. The park, which has an extensive road system, is fenced on only three sides; the fourth boundary is formed by the Athi River, affording access to migrating wildlife. Unfortunately, the area beyond the river – Kitengela, once a traditional Maasai grazing area – is slowly being sold for housing, which is seriously hindering the annual dry-season migration into and out of the park.

Most of the park consists of open grassy plains and scattered acacia bush, intersected by a number of small seasonal rivers and the permanent Athi River, lined by lovely yellow-barked acacia trees, as well as a number of man-made dams holding permanent water. In the west of the park there is an extensive area of highland forest containing olive and Cape chestnut trees.

Nairobi National Park is perhaps the best place in Kenya to see the endangered black rhino, which occur here in good numbers and are quite tame. The black rhino have been so successful here that many have been translocated to other national parks and wildlife areas. The park is also a good

Black rhino

place to see and photograph Africa's largest antelope, the eland, which, unusually, are not at all shy or skittish here. Masai giraffe, buffalo, warthog and both Thomson's and Grant's gazelle are all common. Lion and cheetah both occur and leopards are occasionally seen in the highland forest. Strangely, spotted hyena are seldom encountered, but silver-backed (called black-backed in Southern Africa) jackal do occur. The only major mammal that is not seen here is the elephant, although a few years ago three young males did try to enter the park.

During the dry season (July–October) there is a large influx of wildlife – mainly wildebeest, kongoni (Coke's hartebeest) and zebra – from the Athi-Kapiti Plains into the park. There is a nature trail along the Athi River, which is a wonderful place to walk, especially for birders.

Black rhino (Swahili: *kifaru*)

Rhinos are large, almost prehistoric-looking animals whose numbers have drastically declined during the last 20 years or so. The black rhino is the smaller of the two rhino species, but still weighs an impressive 900–1364kg (2000–3000lb). The average size of its horn varies from 50–90cm (19–35in) for the front horn to just over 50cm (19in) for the rear horn. The average weight of a horn is 2.75–3.5kg (6–8lb).

Black rhino live for 35–40 years and have a gestation period of 15–16 months; only one calf is born. A female produces a calf only about once every four years, which is nursed for one to two years. Because of their low numbers (due to poaching and habitat loss), it is feared that the remaining rhino are so widely dispersed that it is difficult for them to find each other and breed.

Black rhino are browsers with a distinctive pointed prehensile upper lip (while white rhinos are grazers with wide, square lips). They eat a large variety of plants, leaves and plant shoots forming the bulk of their diet.

Rhinos live in home ranges that sometimes overlap those of other individuals, especially at water holes and wallows. These territories are marked by urine spraying and dung heaps; the dung is scattered by the hind feet. Black rhinos are usually solitary, but a female will be accompanied by her latest calf until

Rhino Horn

A rhino's horn, which is not a true horn, is composed of keratin (just like human hair and fingernails) and is not attached to the skull. This horn fetches very high prices. At one time the biggest market for it was North Yemen, where it was mostly used to make the handles of traditional daggers called *Jambiya*. Today the largest market for the horn is China and the Far East, where it is considered an essential ingredient in traditional cures for many illnesses, and as an aphrodisiac. Tests have been carried out to determine if rhino horn does have any fever-reducing effects and it was discovered that if rhino horn was taken in very high dosages it did in fact reduce fever – but aspirin is more effective!

Opposite: Visitors in Nairobi National Park, in a London taxi, watch zebra feeding, with the skyline of the city in the background.

Nairobi National Park

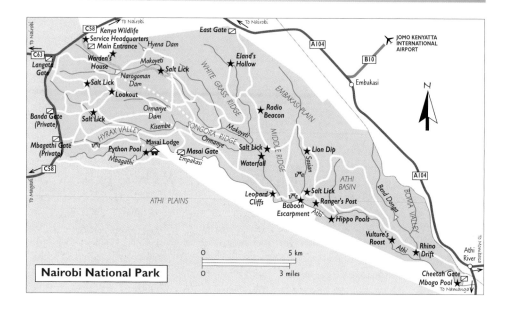

Nairobi National Park

the calf is about three to four years old. When on the move, black rhino calves follow their mothers; this is in contrast to white rhino whose calves always walk in front of their mothers. Their eyesight is very poor, but their hearing and smell are extremely good. This is probably why black rhinos are notoriously ill-tempered and will often charge without apparent reason. For their size black rhinos are very agile and are able to turn quickly, even on the run.

Rhinos are often found with oxpeckers (sometimes called tick birds) on their backs. The birds warn the rhino of danger with a hissing call, and in exchange they feed off the ticks and parasites found on the rhino. In Swahili these birds are called *askari wa kifaru*, which means 'the rhino's guard'.

Oxpeckers (Swahili: *askari wa kifaru*)

Two species of oxpecker occur in Kenya: Red-billed and Yellow-billed. Both accompany large animals and also livestock that have not been treated for ticks. Oxpeckers feed mainly on ticks and blood-sucking flies that they find on their hosts; they comb the hair (in a scissoring action) of their host with a specially shaped (laterally flattened) bill. They also have sharp claws and a very stiff

Oxpeckers

tail that assists them in clinging on to their hosts, especially when the host is moving. As well as feeding on ticks, they also keep wounds clear by eating dead skin and sometimes living flesh. Oxpeckers feed deep in the noses of their hosts and also feed on ear wax. In some parts of southern Africa oxpeckers were eliminated because farmers thought they harmed their livestock. Unfortunately, the livestock then suffered from excessive ear wax and there is now a big movement to reintroduce oxpeckers to those areas again!

Oxpeckers spend most of their time on their hosts; they feed, rest, preen, court, copulate and even occasionally sleep on them (mostly on giraffe, but not buffalo) at night. They pluck their host's fur and use their dung for nests, which are usually in a tree hole or among rocks. Oxpeckers are found in small groups of four to six, but occasionally as many as 20 can be seen feeding on a single, presumably sick, animal. They are co-operative breeders – all of the group will help to feed and rear any young. Red-billed Oxpeckers mostly feed on giraffe, hippo and antelope, such as impala, while Yellow-billed prefer buffalo, rhino, eland, zebra and warthog. Perhaps strangely, they are only very rarely seen on elephants – probably elephants will not tolerate them and can easily sweep them off with their trunk. The few records of oxpeckers seen feeding on elephant have all been associated with sick animals.

Below: A Red-billed Oxpecker clinging to a rhino's head. Oxpeckers feed on ticks, blood-sucking flies and body tissue. In return they act as lookouts for their hosts.

In return for living off a mammal host, oxpeckers act as lookouts. Hunters do not like oxpeckers for this reason; when a hunter (human or animal) is seen, the oxpeckers quickly fly into the sky, scolding loudly as they do so. This can work both ways. Hearing the sound of oxpeckers while walking through long grass can act as an alarm. If they had carried on walking, they might have walked into a solitary old male buffalo, which could have resulted in dire consequences!

Nairobi National Park

Above: A herd of female eland in the Nairobi National Park. These normally shy mammals allow visitors to Nairobi National Park a much closer view than almost anywhere else.

Both species of oxpecker are mainly brown, but Red-billed Oxpeckers, as their name suggests, have a bright red bill and red eyes surrounded by broad yellow eye rings. Yellow-billed Oxpeckers have a yellow bill, tipped in bright red, and bright red eyes. Although their body colour is very similar to that of Red-bills, Yellow-bills have a distinctive paler lower back and rump, which is particularly obvious in flight.

Eland (Swahili: *pouf* or *mbunja*)

The largest of all the antelope, large 1.63m (5.3ft) mature males can weigh almost 700kg (1543lb). Even so, they can still leap almost from a standing position to a height of more than 2m (6.5ft), and youngsters have been known to leap over a 3m (10ft) fence. Eland males weigh on average 500–600kg (1103–1323lb) and females 340–445kg (750–981lb). Both males and females have short spiral horns and a dewlap, but females are smaller and more lightly built. Males slowly become darker, turning blue-grey with age as the skin shows through a thinning coat, and their dewlaps enlarge, often hanging below knee level.

Males regularly thrash the ground or bushes with their horns and often end up with a crown of grass, twigs or weeds. Older males make a loud 'clicking' sound as they walk, which can be heard as

Ol-Doinyo Sabuk National Park

far as 2.5km (1.5 miles) away. This clicking sound was once thought to be coming from the joints or hooves, but it is actually made by the tendons in the front legs. This sound warns other eland who will quickly move out of his path!

Eland are gregarious (herds of up to 1000 have been recorded) but their social organization is different from that of other antelope. Old, dominant males are solitary, while other mature males will form small groups of three to four individuals. Adult females form herds, with the size and make-up of the herd changing daily. Then there are nursery groups consisting of a few adult females and calves, which may not necessarily be their own. One unusual feature of their social system is that adult females will jointly defend calves against predators, including lions.

Eland inhabit open plains and wooded country and they both browse and graze, although they mostly browse. They are also known to dig up large bulbs and tuberous fruits with their horns. They are largely independent of water, although will drink regularly if water is present. Normally very shy, eland have the longest flight distance of any gazelle: 300–500m (328–547yd). However, in the Nairobi National Park and, to a lesser extent, in the Masai Mara National Reserve they are more tame, allowing a much closer approach. Despite this, eland are easily domesticated; they can easily be fattened too. Their meat tastes excellent (and is low in cholesterol) and their milk is creamy. So it is perhaps not surprising that Maasai herders often rear young eland in their herds.

Ol-Doinyo Sabuk National Park

Ol-Doinyo Sabuk, a Maasai phrase meaning 'sleeping buffalo', is a forest-covered hill rising from the surrounding plains. There is only one road (a rough track) that winds its way to the summit through dense highland forest. The view from the summit on a clear day is wonderful: Mount Kenya, Kilimanjaro and Nairobi can all be clearly

Ol-Doinyo Sabuk National Park

Location: 50km (31 miles) from Nairobi.
Size: 18km² (7 sq miles).
Altitude: 1524–2146m (5000–7040ft).
Of interest: Dense highland forest and the graves of early settlers in the area, Sir William Northrop Macmillan and his wife.
Accommodation: There is no accommodation at the park. The nearest accommodation is at the Blue Posts Hotel at Thika, e-mail: bluepostshotel@africaonline.co.ke

Ol-Doinyo Sabuk National Park

Amboseli National Park

Location: 240km (149 miles) from Nairobi via Namanga, or 230km (143 miles) via the Mombasa-Emali Road.
Size: 392km² (151 sq miles).
Altitude: 1128m (3700ft).
Of interest: The elephants here, which have been studied by researcher Cynthia Moss and her team for over 30 years.

seen. Approximately halfway along the road is a panoramic bluff that offers wonderful views over the surrounding countryside. Here are three marble plaques set on slabs of rock; they are the graves of Sir William Northrop Macmillan (a famous hunter and philanthropist), his wife and their servant, Louise Decker. Sir William, who loved this view, was one of the early settlers in this area and owned the nearby 8049ha (19,890-acre) Juja Ranch.

Although the park has a good population of wildlife, including buffalo, bushbuck, leopard and beautiful colobus monkeys, it is difficult to see them as the forest is very thick. Many interesting highland forest birds occur here, such as Hartlaub's Turaco, White-starred Forest Robin and the stunning Narina Trogon.

Amboseli National Park

Amboseli National Park, dominated by snow-capped Kilimanjaro that provides a superb backdrop for photographing the wildlife, is Kenya's most visited wildlife area. Although Kilimanjaro seems close, it is actually located 48km (30 miles) away across the border in Tanzania.

Amboseli was originally designated a reserve in 1948 with an area of 3260km² (1259 sq miles). It was handed back to the Maasai in 1961, but because of conflict between the Maasai herds and wildlife, the reserve was gazetted a national park in 1974 (at a fraction of its original size). Now only 392km² (151 sq miles), the park centres on Ol Tukai, the Maasai word for the local phoenix palm that grows in the area. This area is a magnet for wildlife as it contains many swamps fed by subterranean water draining from Kilimanjaro. To compensate the Maasai, who traditionally watered and grazed their livestock in the area, a number of wells were sunk just outside the national park with funds donated by the New York Zoological Society.

Amboseli National Park

Amboseli National Park

Most of the park consists of a dry, ancient lake bed and fragile grasslands with patches of acacia woodland, while in the southern area there are a number of small rocky volcanic hills. Around the swamps – Ol Okenya, Ol Tukai and Enkongo Narok – the vegetation is lush, with yellow-barked acacia trees and phoenix palms. One of Amboseli's big attractions is its elephants (over 1000); it is possibly the best wildlife area in Africa to experience elephants at close range, and many of the bulls have large tusks. These elephants have never been harassed by poachers and to sit and watch them at close range, feeding and drinking in the swamps with Kilimanjaro in the background, is an experience not to be forgotten. Cynthia Moss and Joyce Pool, with their many assistants, have undertaken extensive studies of these elephants. Cynthia herself has followed their movements for over 30 years, the most extended study of any one species by the same person in Africa.

Apart from elephant, the variety of wildlife includes black rhino, buffalo, Masai giraffe, Grant's and Thomson's gazelle, lion, cheetah and leopard. In the dryer areas of the park, away from the swamps, one can see fringe-eared oryx, gerenuk, lesser kudu and eland. Bird life is prolific too, especially in and around the swamps. Both White and Pink-backed Pelicans, various ducks and cormorants share the waters with the beautiful Pygmy Duck, which is an uncommon bird in Kenya. Kingfishers and bee-eaters use the reeds along the swamp to look out for their prey, and birds of prey are well represented, with African Fish Eagle, Martial Eagle, Eastern Chanting Goshawk and the tiny Pygmy Falcon all occurring.

No visit to Amboseli is complete without a visit to Observation Hill. Walk to the top for a sweeping view over the whole of Amboseli spread out below. You will see the dust trails of animals walking across the expanses of dry plains to water and, towards the south, an almost endless tract covered with acacia trees merging into the base of Kilimanjaro. Some days an opportunistic Maasai warrior in full traditional dress will pose, for a small donation, for a photograph with Kilimanjaro in the background.

Elephants (Swahili: *ndovu*)

The African elephant is the largest living land mammal. An adult bull elephant can weigh as much as 6500kg (14,330lb) and be as tall as 3.3m (11ft) at the shoulder. Elephants spend most of their

Accommodation

Amboseli National Park
Amboseli Serena Safari Lodge:
www.serenahotels.com
Amboseli Sopa Lodge:
www.sopalodges.com
Ol Tukai Lodge:
www.oltukailodge.com
Tortilis Camp: www.chelipeacock.com
Outside Amboseli National Park
Kilimanjaro Buffalo Lodge:
www.africansafariclub.com
Kimana Lodge:
www.africansafariclub.com
Porini Camp: www.porini.com/
amboseli_porini_camp.html
Chyulu Hills National Park
Ol Donyo Wuas:
7 individual cottages,
www.RichardBonhamSafaris.com
Campi ya Kanzi:
www.campiyakanzi.com
Ol Kanjau:
www.bush-and-beyond.com
Umanyi Springs Camp:
tel: 0721 317762.

Amboseli National Park

The Amboseli Elephant Research Project

Amboseli's elephants are the best-known elephants in Africa. In 1972 Cynthia Moss initiated a long-term study that is still continuing to this day. The Amboseli elephants were chosen because they were probably the last relatively undisturbed population in Africa. The local Maasai people never hunted elephants and their presence in the area helped deter any poachers! Over 1200 elephants have been identified individually and each has been assigned a name, number or code. There are currently almost 800 individuals and the birth date of well over half of these is known.

time eating – about 5% of their body weight is consumed each day, and each elephant needs 100–227 litres (30–40 gallons) of water. Unfortunately, they only digest about 40% of the vegetation they eat. Although they prefer grass, they also eat leaves, bark, fruit and seed pods. Elephants can go several days without water, but they prefer to drink and bathe daily if water is available. After bathing elephants use their trunks to blow mud or dust over themselves.

Both male and female African elephants have tusks, whereas only male Asian elephants have them. Elephant tusks are actually very long upper incisors, of which a third of their length is inside the skull. The largest tusk recorded weighed 102.7kg (214lb) and its length was 345cm (11.5ft), but nowadays, because of years of hunting and poaching, it is rare to see one that weighs more than 50kg (110lb). Elephants are 'right- or left-tusked' just as humans are right- or left-handed; they use one tusk more than the other, which makes it shorter and often shaped differently from the other. Their teeth are also very unusual: they break out in sequence from front to rear, with only one tooth and part of another tooth in use at one time. They have 12 teeth, which are slowly worn out one after the other, in both the upper and lower jaws. The last teeth are the largest and usually in use by the time an elephant is in its late 40s; these have to last the animal for the rest of its life. When these teeth are worn out, the elephant cannot chew food very well so it slowly starves to death, usually at about 60–70 years of age. It is not unusual to see old bull elephants spending their last days feeding in or near swamps, where the vegetation may be softer and more easily chewed with their worn-out teeth. This may be why it was thought for a long time that elephants had secret burial grounds.

Another remarkable feature of the elephant is its trunk, which is an asset in so many ways. It is a nose, a hand, a tool for gathering food and siphoning up water, for sucking up dust and then blowing it over the body. It can be used in fighting and for pulling down branches, yet it can also be so gentle as to be able to pick up items as small as a pea.

The elephant's ears are large and are used for cooling on hot days. There are many veins in an elephant's ear and on hot days you can see elephants slowly fanning their ears. This motion helps circulate the blood, which is cooled by about 13°C (9°F) when it returns to the body.

Yet another unusual feature is the female elephant's teats. She has two teats located on her chest between the front legs, which is very different from all other herbivores.

Elephants are gregarious, forming groups that are made up of related females and their young. These groups are led by an old matriarch. At one time it was thought that elephant groups were led by an old bull, but bulls spend most of their time alone or with other bulls, only visiting the groups to check if any of the females are in oestrus. The gestation period is approximately 22 months and usually only one calf is born. Calves nurse for two to four years, using their mouth with the trunk held over the head. It is not unusual to see quite young calves picking up grass and putting it into their mouths. Calves also often reach up and take food out of their mothers' mouths, which may be how young elephants learn what is good to eat. When drinking water, a young calf has to kneel down and drink using its mouth – it is some time before it learns to draw the water up into its trunk and then pour it into its mouth.

Below: Three of Amboseli's tuskers head out of the park at sunset to feed at night. It is a regular occurrence for Amboseli's elephants to feed outside the park at night.

Amboseli National Park

Female calves mature at about 11–12 years of age and stay with their group, while males do not mature until they are 12–15 years of age and are then usually expelled from the herd. This separation is usually a gradual process, with the young bull remaining close to its maternal group. But gradually the females become more and more intolerant of them and they become completely independent, joining up with other males to form bachelor groups. Mature bulls come into musth (a time when their testosterone levels are high – a phase of heightened sexual activity and aggression) when they are about 25–30 years old and wander alone, occasionally joining up with the female groups in case any of the females are in oestrus. During this period, which may last a week or even a month, the male secretes a strong-smelling thick liquid from its temporal glands and dribbles very strong-smelling urine.

Fringe-eared oryx (Swahili: *choroa*)

The fringe-eared oryx is one of two subspecies of oryx that occur in Kenya. The fringe-eared is found south of the Tana River (including at Amboseli) and in northern Tanzania, while the other subspecies, the beisa oryx, is found north of the Tana River and into Somalia and Ethiopia. Fringe-eared oryx differ from beisa in having long, distinctive tassels on the end of their ears and heavier, darker brown coats. Oryx are large antelope with long, spear-like horns and have adapted to living in hot, dry areas. In the arid areas where they live, some of the plants that oryx feed on have adapted to store water or to prevent the excessive loss of it. The marked difference between day and night temperatures causes dew to form which is absorbed by the plant; some plants increase their water content by 25–40%, so the oryx that feed on them get both food and water. This allows an oryx to go without drinking for weeks and, if necessary, months, although where water is available they will drink every few days. Both sexes have horns but those of the females are usually longer and thinner than those of the males. The horns are straight and almost parallel and can be as long as 76cm (30in); the record length is more than a metre (39in). Oryx are remarkably dexterous with their horns – they can easily scratch their backs with them, and can also use them to fend off predators such as lion and leopard. They have even been known to thrust their horns completely through a lion. They are very nomadic, presumably because of their harsh environment, and live in gregarious herds of mixed sexes, numbering 10 to 40 but, occasionally, as large as 200.

Yellow baboon

Yellow baboon
(Swahili: *nyani*)

Two types of baboon occur in Kenya: the olive baboon and the yellow baboon. The olive baboon inhabits western and central Kenya, while the yellow baboon can be found in the southern and coastal areas of Kenya. Yellow baboons are smaller, slimmer and lighter in colour and are far less common than olive baboons.

Baboons are extremely social, living in well-organized groups, known as troops, which can number from 40 to 80 members. Each troop (on average 50 individuals) is led by a dominant male who is much larger than the female. Females outnumber males and form the social core of the group, remaining with it all their lives. Young males leave their troop as they become mature and spend time with other troops. When a young male joins a troop he spends most of the time on the edge, interacting with different females until he is accepted into the troop. Within a troop some females are of a higher ranking than others and their young take on this status. Lower-ranking females have to defer to the young of a higher-ranking female, even if it is an infant.

Above: One of Amboseli's yellow baboons. These baboons have been extensively studied by researchers over a number of years.

An infant baboon has a pink face and black fur and for the first month of its life it stays very close to its mother, hanging below her stomach as she travels. By 5–6 weeks old the babies can ride on their mothers' backs, hanging on tightly with their hands and feet. After a few months they can ride jockey-style, sitting upright on her back and supported by her tail. From 4–6 months old the young baboon slowly changes colour to dark brown and spends more time with other juveniles; young baboons are suckled for about a year.

Amboseli National Park

Ceremonial Rites

No Maasai ceremony takes place without a bull, an ox or a cow, as the animal's blood plays an important role: while the animal's head is tightly held, the jugular vein is cut using the tip of an arrow or by shooting the arrow directly into the vein (the arrow has a leather thong wrapped around it just behind its tip to prevent it from penetrating too far). Once the blood has been collected in a gourd, the vein is simply pinched and plugged with a wad of dung and mud. The blood is usually mixed with milk, but is also drunk untainted by warriors, by women who have just given birth, or by a person who has undergone circumcision rites.

Baboons live for 20–30 years. Their main predator outside of protected areas is man, but otherwise leopards are their main enemy. Male baboons are fierce, and a group of males will chase off a single leopard or even a lion. Baboons are omnivorous and eat a large selection of food, and although grass forms a large part of their diet, they also eat seeds, berries, pods, blossoms, roots, bark and sap. They eat ants, termites and grasshoppers and have been recorded eating small mammals such as hares, as well as birds, fish and shellfish. Some males have been known to specialize in hunting young gazelle and goats if the opportunity arises.

Right: A Maasai Moran (warrior) wearing an Enkisi-au (lion headdress) signifying that he has killed a lion.

The Maasai people

The Maasai people

The Maasai are pastoralists, herding their cattle, sheep and goats; they also keep donkeys as beasts of burden. The majority of the Maasai still remain firmly attached to their traditional way of life. Second only to their children, the most important aspect of their lives is cattle, which they believe were given to them by their god Enkai; a Maasai of modest wealth will own at least 50. (He will, however, only be considered wealthy if he also has children.) The beasts are rarely slaughtered for meat (special ceremonial occasions aside). Instead they provide the Maasai people with all their needs: milk and blood for nourishment, hides for bedding and for making sandals, and as payment in the case of a dowry or fine.

The Maasai live in an *enk'ang* (often wrongly called a *manyatta*), which is a collection of huts housing Maasai warriors. Low, igloo-shaped huts are constructed by the women out of thin branches and grass, which they cover with a mixture of cow dung and mud. The *enk'ang* is surrounded by a strong thorn-bush fence, and each evening cattle, sheep and goats belonging to all the families are herded into this enclosure until morning. The huts are usually divided into two or three alcoves: one is used as a sleeping area for very young calves, lambs and kids; the others form the Maasai sleeping areas and cooking area.

A cultural feature of Maasai life is the male's passage through four traditional phases, each one marked by an important ceremony. The first one, called the *alamal lengipaata*, is performed just before circumcision. Because the circumcision ceremony only takes place every 12 to 15 years, the age of the boys taking part in the rites varies considerably. At this time, the group picks one of its members as a leader, who then retains the title throughout the lives of people in that particular group. The first phase is followed by *emorata*, or circumcision, initiating the boys into warriorhood. During the ceremony, the boys may show no sign of pain; to do so would be a disgrace. After a period of healing, they become warriors and are known as *morans*. They then become junior elders through the ceremony of *eunoto*, after which they may marry. Finally, with the *olngesherr* ceremony, they become senior elders whose duties are to preside over Maasai affairs. Traditionally the Maasai have no chiefs or headmen; all decisions are made by the senior elders.

Circumcision and Marriage Rites

Maasai girls are circumcised at puberty. Although a ceremony is held, it is limited to family as girls are not separated into age groups; circumcision takes place in the mother's house. Like the boys, the Maasai girls dress in black robes smeared with oil, and around their heads they wear a band with long links of metal beads hanging from it to cover their eyes. After circumcision the girls are allowed to marry, but because men may only enter into marriage once they become elders, the girls' husbands are normally much older than they are.

Passage to Manhood

Once male circumcision has taken place, a period of healing follows during which the boys daub their faces white and wear black robes. They use a small bow to shoot birds, which are fashioned into a special headdress – this is one way in which to prove their manhood and skills. A headdress can have as many as 50 birds. These circumcised young men travel all over Maasailand, and at the end of this period, the warriors grow their hair long, cover their bodies with ochre and dress in their finery.

CHYULU HILLS, TSAVO EAST AND TSAVO WEST

The two Tsavo national parks and the adjoining Chyulu Hills National Park make up one Africa's largest wildlife areas. Tsavo West has spectacular scenery with soaring mountains and the famous Mzima Springs. Kilimanjaro is also visible on a clear day. Tsavo East, by contrast, is a plateau of open thorn bush country with wonderful giant baobab trees, where the Yatta Plateau, the world's longest lava flow, 300km (186 miles) long, dominates the skyline.

The Chyulu Hills are of recent volcanic origin and offer the visitor the chance to walk or take horse rides accompanied with experienced guides. The views from the Chyulus can be quite spectacular with Kilimanjaro seeming to float above the terrain in the distance.

Top Ten

Hirola
Lesser kudu
Klipspringer
Yellow baboon
Striped hyena
Black rhino (Ngulia Sanctuary)
'Red' Elephants
Hippo (view under water at
    Mzima Springs)
Golden-breasted Starling
Rosy-patched Shrike

Opposite, top to bottom: A group of female (and one male) waterbuck in the Chyulu Hills National Park; the beautiful clear water of the Tsavo River near its source at Mzima Springs; in the dry season, herds of animals congregate at a water hole in Tsavo East.

Chyulu Hills National Park

**Chyulu Hills
National Park**

Location: 200km (124 miles)
from Nairobi.
Size: 471km² (182 sq miles).
Altitude: 2170m (7120ft).
Of interest: Wonderful walks with
great views. Here the popular house
plants African violets can be found
growing in the wild.
Accommodation: *Chyulu Hills (self-
catering three-bedroom guesthouse
near the park):* tourism@kws.org
See also panel, page 33.

The Chyulu Hills, lying to the east of Amboseli and running
parallel with the Nairobi-to-Mombasa road for 80km (50 miles),
became a national park in 1983. The park comprises several
hundred small, grass-covered volcanic hills that are only some
400–500 years old, and a number of beautiful forested valleys. It
is possible to walk along the crest of these hills, from where the
views of Kilimanjaro and the surrounding countryside are
phenomenal. There is also a very rough track through the hills,
negotiable with a four-wheel-drive vehicle. It is thought that rainfall
percolating through the Chyulus feeds the famous Mzima Springs in
nearby Tsavo West National Park. A variety of wildlife occurs in
the area, including fringed-eared oryx, elephant, Masai giraffe,
Coke's hartebeest (kongoni), lion and cheetah. Over 400 species
of birds have been recorded here.

Tsavo National Park

This very large wildlife area is larger than Wales and about the
same size as the states of New Hampshire and Vermont combined.
It has an area of 20,810km² (8035 sq miles) and varies in altitude
from 230–2000m (755–6562ft). The Nairobi-to-Mombasa road

Tsavo National Park

splits the park into two halves: Tsavo East and Tsavo West national parks. Since the park was split mainly for administration purposes, the two areas differ markedly. Tsavo East consists of miles of flat, dry thornbush interspersed with magnificent baobab trees and dominated by the 300km long (186-mile) Yatta Plateau, the world's longest lava flow. Although it is dry thornbush country, the vista is of volcanic mountains, hills and outcrops, with magnificent views. Along the Tsavo River there is lush vegetation, comprising doum palms, tamarind and acacia trees. For much of the year Tsavo burns dry and dusty; the red Tsavo dust blankets everything, including the elephants, which are known here for their red colour. Once numbering tens of thousands, drought and serious poaching in the late 70s and early 80s have severely reduced the elephant population, now standing at around 5000–6000. However, their destructive effect on the environment has been lessened as a result, and the vegetation is recovering, in many places thicker than before. After rain Tsavo transforms almost overnight – the grasses push up fresh shoots and many colourful wildflowers, such as the pink and white convolvulus, quickly appear.

Klipspringer (Swahili: *mbuzi mawe*)

This is a small antelope usually found in pairs on kopjes and rocky outcrops. Klipspringers have a very thick coat which is stiff and brittle, unlike any other African antelope. They stand on the tips of their hooves, which are specially adapted for their life on rocks. Klipspringers are very sure-footed and appear to bounce from rock to rock. They are capable of extraordinary jumps and make rapid progress from rock to rock without apparent footholds. In East Africa both males and females have horns but in other parts of Africa only the males have horns.

Klipspringers find all their food, mostly sparse grass and herbs that grow among the rocks, where they live and can manage without water for long periods. The best time to see klipspringers is in the early mornings when they can be seen standing out in the open; they spend the rest of the day lying down in the shade.

Lesser kudu (Swahili: *tandala dogo*)

These shy antelope are smaller and more graceful than greater kudu and have more stripes (11–15) on their flanks. Lesser kudu

Tsavo's Red Elephants

Tsavo's elephants are often referred to as 'red elephants'. Actually the elephants of Tsavo are no different in colour from any other elephants; it's just that the soil in Tsavo is very red in colour and when they bathe or dust themselves they quickly take on the colour of the red soil! Tsavo's red elephants, at one time numbering around 50,000, have dramatically changed the vegetation in the area. During a very severe drought in the late 60s and early 70s, the elephants ate virtually all the available vegetation and badly damaged many of the baobab trees. Together with black rhino, they died of starvation in large numbers. Ironically, before the drought the elephants were the subject of much debate on the issue of culling but, before any decisions were made, nature took its course. Since that time the vegetation has made a remarkable recovery and the elephants are increasing in numbers too.

Opposite: The beautiful Chyulu Hills are some of the youngest mountains in the world. They were formed only a few hundred years ago. On the southwestern side of the Chyulus is the evil-looking black Shaitani (Swahili for devil) lava flow. Surprisingly, black rhino occur in this inhospitable habitat.

Tsavo East National Park

Tsavo East National Park

Location: 200km (124 miles) from Nairobi.

Size: 11,747km² (4534 sq miles).

Altitude: 230–975m (755–3200ft).

Of interest: Lugard's Falls , and the rare and endangered hirola antelope.

Accommodation:

Galdessa Camp: www.galdessa.com

Satao Camp: www.sataocamp.com

Patterson's Camp: pattersons@iconnect.co.ke

Voi Safari Lodge: www.voilodge.kenya-safari.co.ke

Crocodile Camp: www.africasafariclub.com

Taita Hill Lodge and Salt Lick Lodge (situated between Tsavo East and West): www.saltlicklodge.com

Hilton Hotels: www.hilton.com

Taita Discovery Centre: www.originsafaris.info

Ngutuni Lodge (situated in its own sanctuary adjacent to Tsavo East): ngutunilodge@wananchi.com

also have two conspicuous white patches: one on the upper, and the other on the lower part of the neck. Only the males have horns, which are long and spiralled. Lesser kudu live in much dryer country and can survive without water for a long time. They live in small groups of one to three females and their young, while males are mostly solitary. Immature males leave the family groups and for a while join other young males until they are more mature, at about four or five years old. Lesser kudu prefer dense riverine thickets where they are very difficult to see; here they browse on leaves, seed pods and fruits. When disturbed they take flight with large leaps and with their tails curled over their backs.

Red-billed Hornbill (Swahili: *hondohondo*)

This is one of the characteristic birds of the dry bush country and its call, a monotonous 'kok kok kok', is a very common sound of the bush. They are usually found in pairs, often feeding on the ground on seeds and insects such as scorpions and beetles. The male and female are very similar, but the females are smaller and have a shorter beak. Their display is interesting: pairs duet with their wings partially open and their heads bowed; they bob up and down, and at the same time the calling gets faster and faster. Their nesting, like other hornbills (except the Ground Hornbill), is unusual: they nest in a hole in a tree. After mating, the female seals herself in a tree hole with mud, leaving a small slit through which she is fed by the male. The female stays here for the whole of the incubation period. During this time she undergoes a moult, growing new feathers, and continues to be fed by the male. When the eldest of the chicks is about 21 days old the female breaks out of the nest and helps the male feed the growing young.

Scarlet-chested Sunbird

Sunbirds occupy a similar niche in Africa to the hummingbirds of the Americas. Most have long bills with which they probe blossoms. Males can be very pugnacious especially during the breeding season. Scarlet-chested Sunbirds can very often be seen feeding on non-indigenous flowers planted in the gardens of safari lodges. Males perch on prominent branches showing off their bright scarlet chests.

Tsavo East National Park

Most of Tsavo East north of the Galana River is closed to the public; only a few professional safari companies are allowed to enter. The park has a very good network of well-signposted roads and tracks and, because the terrain is mostly dry, flat thornbush scrub (the mountain and hills of Tsavo West are missing here) and there are fewer visitors, it has an aura of untamed Africa. The monotonous scrub is occasionally broken by green vegetation along the Galana River and the small seasonal rivers that cross the area.

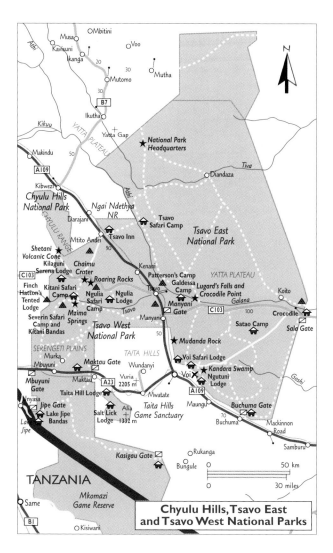

Chyulu Hills, Tsavo East and Tsavo West National Parks

Tsavo East National Park

Hirola or Hunter's Hartebeest (Swahili: *hirola*)

This antelope is similar to a hartebeest, but larger, measuring 99cm (39in) at the shoulder and weighing about 73kg (160lb). Hirola are slimmer-looking and both male and females have long, slender horns, which are very similar to impala horns. Hirola are pale brown in colour with a distinctive white chevron between the eyes and a long hairy tail. They are grazers and can survive without water.

Below: Lugard's Falls are remarkable for the fantastic shapes of their rocks.

The most interesting area to visit is that around Voi, the park's headquarters. Dominated by Voi Safari Lodge set high on a bluff, the Kandara Swamp and Voi River lie to the east. The vegetation is rich along the swamp and river and it is here that most of the wildlife occurs. Also in this area you may be lucky and come across a herd of Daphne Sheldrick's orphaned elephants. To the north of the lodge is Mudanda Rock, a miniature of Australia's Ayres Rock. Two kilometres long (1.2 miles), it stands out prominently from the surrounding plains. Below the rock a natural water hole attracts a great deal of wildlife, particularly during the dry season. There is a parking area to the western side of the rock and a footpath leads to a spot from where one can climb up to the top. From here the views over the plains are wonderful and occasionally one can see elephants and other mammals drinking there.

About 60km (37 miles) north of Voi are Lugard's Falls (named after Captain Lugard, Britain's first proconsul in East Africa) on the Galana River. The falls, actually a series of rapids, are most dramatic and impressive after rain, when the river's flow is constricted in the narrow rocky gorge. Below the falls very large crocodiles can usually be seen at Crocodile Point. Wildlife found here is similar to that found at Tsavo West, but in the area of Satao Camp you have a good chance of seeing the highly endangered hirola antelope (Hunter's hartebeest), relocated here from the border with Somalia in 1996. Tsavo East is good for dryland birds such as the stunning Golden-breasted Starling, Orange-bellied Parrot and the odd-looking Vulturine Guineafowl.

Hirola Conservation

The hirola, also known as Hunter's hartebeest, is one of Africa's most endangered antelope. It is a relative of the hartebeest but has adapted to live in more arid areas. The hirola's range was originally restricted to a small area straddling the Kenya/Somalia border. At some time in the 1970s there was a drastic decline in its population and by 1995 only 300 of the animals were thought to survive in a very small area of southeastern Kenya (the hirola's status in Somalia is unknown). In 1963 a number of hirola (about 20) were moved to Tsavo East National Park and by 1996 they had increased to approximately 80 individuals. In 1995 the

Tsavo West National Park

Hirola Management Committee (HMC) was formed with a
mandate to conserve the species. In 1996 a further 29 hirola
were translocated to Tsavo East National Park and it is now
estimated that there are at least 100 individuals. It must be said
that the local people in Ljara are now very protective of 'their'
antelope and it took some skilful negotiations by KWS to allow
them to move the 29 hirola to Tsavo West National Park.

Tsavo West National Park

Tsavo West National Park is predominantly semi-arid plains
broken with granite outcrops and lava fields. The highest and
most magnificent, Ngulia Mountain is 1830m (almost 6000ft) high.
Tsavo West is the most visited section in Tsavo National Park,
offering many attractions apart from its wildlife. The foremost
is the famous Mzima Springs where up to 227.3 million litres
(50 million gallons) of cool, crystal-clear water flows out of the
ground through the porous volcanic rocks. This water is believed
to originate from the Chyulu Hills via an underground river.
Water from the springs is piped all the way (150km; 95 miles) to
the city of Mombasa on the coast. At Mzima there is a car park
and visitors are permitted to walk to the springs' source and
along a pathway which follows the water. The walk is a wonderful
experience. If you are quiet you may be rewarded with the sight
of animals and birds coming down to the water's edge to drink,
and you are sure to see hippos clearly as they lie in the cool clear
water. One can also watch for hippos through the windows of an
observation tank sunk into the river, which allows the visitor to
enter a cool, new underwater world. Swimming close to the
tank's windows are likely to be a number of fish, mostly barbel
species. Troops of black-faced vervet monkeys and many
interesting birds inhabit the trees around Mzima. This is also
one of the few places in Kenya where darters can be seen.

Other interesting places to visit include the Roaring Rocks, which
get their name from the sound made by the wind that blows
through them. Here, from the top of a 98m (300ft) rock face,
there are wonderful views over Tsavo; similar views can be
experienced from Poacher's Lookout. The volcanic Chaimu
Crater, less than 200 years old and composed of black coke, is
well worth visiting and can be climbed if you are interested. This

**Tsavo West
National Park**

Location: 200km (124 miles)
from Nairobi.

Size: 9065km² (3500 sq miles).

Altitude: 229–2000m
(750–6560ft).

Accommodation:

Finch Hatton's: www.finchhattons.com

Kilaguni Serena Lodge:
www.serenahotels.com

Ngulia Lodge: www.kenya-safari.co.ke
or www.ngulialodge.kenya-safari.co.ke

Voyager Zawani Luxury Tented
Camp: www.heritagehotels.com

Severin Safari Camp:
www.severin-kenya.com

Kitani Bandas (self-catering): tel 041
5485 0015 or book through Severin.

Ngulia Self-service Bandas:
www.kws.org

Tsavo West National Park

Man-eaters of Tsavo

This is the title of a true account, written by Colonel JH Patterson, who was in charge of building a bridge over the Tsavo River for the Uganda Railway in 1898. For some time, workers were continually being dragged off into the night by two large male lions; the workers believed it was the Devil in the shape of a lion, as the lions were quite fearless. Eventually, in December 1898, after a mounting death toll including 28 Indian workers and a large number of Africans, work on the bridge was brought to a halt until the lions were shot. After many nights of waiting, Colonel Patterson shot the lions. These lions are on display in the Chicago Natural History Museum.

area is a good place to look out for klipspringer (see page 43). It is also a good place for lesser kudu. Other wildlife found in Tsavo include lion, leopard, cheetah, elephant, Masai giraffe, eland, fringe-eared oryx, buffalo, Burchell's zebra, yellow baboon, Coke's hartebeest and Grant's gazelle. Below Ngulia Mountain there is a well-guarded Rhino Sanctuary containing a number of black rhino.

In the southwest corner of Tsavo West is Lake Jipe, 10km (6 miles) long and 3km (1.9 miles) wide, which has the Kenya/Tanzania border bisecting it. Above the lake, the Tanzanian Pare Mountains form a dramatic backdrop, especially at sunset. On clear days, Kilimanjaro can be seen towards the northwest. Although there are a good variety of mammals in the area, it is the bird life that attracts most visitors. The lake shore is the best place in Kenya to see Purple Gallinule, Black Herons, Pygmy Goose and, occasionally, Lesser Jacana.

Hippopotamus (Swahili: *kibiko*)

After the elephant and white rhino, the hippo is the third largest mammal – a full-grown male can weigh up to 3200kg (7040lb). The name hippopotamus comes from the Greek *hippos*, meaning 'horse'; in Roman days they were called 'river horses'. Until recently hippos were thought to be closely related to the pig family but recent research using DNA has shown them to be more closely related to whales!

Hippos live in groups of typically 10 to 15, but at times of low water more will crowd together. The resonant honking made by submerged hippos is one of the most familiar and impressive African wildlife sounds. Hippos close both their eyes and nostrils when they submerge, and mature hippos can stay underwater for up to five minutes, but on average they only stay submerged for a minute and a half.

Dominant males control a section of a river or lake shore and tolerate other males as long as they are submissive. At times, though, they drive out other males with great rage, inflicting deep gashes on each other, and they will even attack young males and are known to kill hippo calves. The so called hippo 'yawn' is

Hippopotamus

actually a threat display, usually given by a dominant male, showing off his long, formidable razor-sharp incisors and tusk-like canines. Hippos are very unpredictable; if they are encountered away from the safety of water, anything that gets in the way of them returning to water may be attacked. Many serious accidents have resulted from these encounters.

Hippos feed at night and rest by day in the water. Shortly after nightfall, or earlier if they feel safe, hippos leave the river or lake on well-worn paths, walking for up to 2.8km (1.7 miles), grazing as they go, and return to the river before dawn. During droughts when feed is in short supply they will often delay their return until a few hours after dawn and, in extreme times, will stay out all day seeking shelter from the sun in thick vegetation. Hippos feed on short grass, eating up to 40kg (88lb) a night, using their muscular wide (up to 50cm/20in) lips. Hippos spend most of the day in water shallow enough for them to lie on their bellies with their short legs tucked under, but if there is little human disturbance they will lie out on the bank in the morning sun.

Mating takes place in the water but births usually take place in shallow water with the female partially out of the water. If born in the water the newborn is helped to the surface by the mother. At first a young hippo, which can weigh 25–55kg (55–121lb) at birth, cannot swim, and climbs up onto its mother's neck or back to rest. Young hippos can suckle underwater – they close their nostrils and ears then wrap their tongue tightly around their mother's teat. After about three months young hippos begin to eat grass but continue to suckle until about eight months old. Calves are often left in crèches where they engage in play fights and chase each other around.

Taita Hills Game Sanctuary

Location: 40km (25 miles) west of Voi.

Size: 113km² (44 sq miles).

Altitude: 914m (3000ft).

Of interest: This sanctuary is privately owned and run by the Hilton Hotel chain. This area was once an abandoned sisal plantation which has been transformed into an exciting wildlife reserve containing a large variety of wildlife.

Below: A hippo seen underwater from the windows of the observation tank at Mzima Springs in Tsavo West National Park.

SHIMBA HILLS, MWALANGANJE AND TANA RIVER

The Shimba Hills National Reserve and the adjoining Mwalanganje Elephant Sanctuary are the closest wildlife areas for visitors staying at the beach resorts in the Mombasa area. For these visitors it is just a short drive to experience a part of real wild Africa.

By contrast, the Tana River Primate National Reserve is only for the experienced Africa travellers who are self-sufficient with regard to food, water and fuel. To get there requires a long, hot drive along unmade and mostly unmarked roads.

Top Ten

Sable antelope (Shimba Hills)

Elephants (Shimba Hills)

Cycads (Shimba Hills)

Palm-nut Vulture (Shimba Hills)

Fischer's Turaco (Shimba Hills)

Crested mangabey (only 800 left, Tana River)

Red colobus (Tana River)

Northern Carmine Bee-eater (Shimba Hills and coastal mangroves)

Crested Guineafowl (Tana River)

Pel's Fishing Owl (Tana River)

Opposite, top to bottom:
A dhow off the coast; the rolling forested hills of the Shimba Hills National Reserve; a female elephant feeding with her young at Shimba Hills.

Shimba Hills National Reserve

**Shimba Hills
National Reserve**

Location: 540km (336 miles) from
Nairobi, 56km (35 miles) from
Mombasa.
Size: 320km² (124 sq miles).
Altitude: 120–450m (394–1476ft).
Of interest: Kenya's last herd of
sable antelope, elephants, and ancient
cycads. Be sure to spend a night at
Shimba's tree lodge.
Accommodation:
Shimba Lodge:
Shimba@aberdaresafarihotels.com
www.aberdaresafarihotels.com

Shimba Hills National Reserve

Shimba Hills National Reserve was established in 1968 to protect
one of the last breeding herds of sable antelope in Kenya and to
protect a herd of roan antelope that had originally been
introduced from an area near Thika, north of Nairobi.
Unfortunately, the roan were unable to adapt to their new home
and different vegetation and they died out. During the 1990s
Masai giraffe were introduced; these have been successful and
they are now fully assimilated into this environment.

The reserve consists of rolling hills and forest, with wonderful
views of the Indian Ocean. The forest is one of the largest areas
of coastal rainforest in East Africa. Mammals to be found here
include elephant, buffalo, Burchell's zebra, common waterbuck,
lion and leopard. Bird life is good, too; among the more
interesting species that can be seen here are the Palm-nut
Vulture, Southern Banded Snake Eagle, Grasshopper Buzzard,
both Trumpeter and Silvery-cheeked Hornbills, Carmine Bee-
eaters, Green-headed Oriole and Fischer's Turaco. Nearby is
the Mwalanganje Elephant Sanctuary.

Mwalanganje Elephant Sanctuary

This 24,282ha (60,000-acre) sanctuary is a community-owned
wildlife area located adjacent to the Shimba Hills National Reserve.
It was established in 1995 by the local Mwalanganje community

*Right: A herd of sable antelope
in the Shimba Hills National
Reserve, the only area where
these beautiful mammals
occur in Kenya.*

Mwalanganje Elephant Sanctuary

with help from the KWS, the US Agency for International
Development (through its Conservation of Biodiverse Resource
Areas program), the Born Free Foundation and the Eden Wildlife
Trust. The sanctuary was set up to create a corridor for the
movement of elephants from the Shimba Hills to the Mwalanganje
Forest Reserve, and is surrounded by an electric fence.

For many years elephants have traditionally passed through the
area, migrating between the Shimba Hills and the surrounding
areas. In the late 1980s the elephants started occupying the area
more and more, which caused conflict between the elephants and
the local people, and as the elephants started destroying crops
the farmers retaliated by killing the elephants. To resolve this
situation, more than 200 families voluntarily contributed land to
the sanctuary, agreeing not to farm it. In return, they became
shareholders and managers of the Elephant Sanctuary and
received annual dividends from tourism. The local people were
also given jobs as rangers and guides.

The Mwalanganje Elephant Sanctuary is the first ever community-
owned conservation enterprise dedicated to the protection of
the elephant. It has helped to minimize human/wildlife conflicts
in the area and has enhanced the socio-cultural and economic
well-being of the local community. Apart from elephant, sable
antelope, bushbuck, impala, warthog and leopard are also present.
Other attraction are the beautiful Kitsanze Waterfall, as well as
rare cycads (*cycadaceae*), a primitive group of plants which
flourished over 200 million years ago.

Too Many Elephants

Over the years the elephant
population has grown causing
problems when they raid local farms.
Because of this conflict a decision was
made to reduce their number by
moving some to Tsavo National Park.
During 2005 KWS transferred 150
elephants from Shimba Hills National
Park to Tsavo East National Park, and
more followed in 2006. Elephants are
darted in family units and transferred
by specially adapted trucks to Tsavo.
This is the biggest transfer of elephants
ever undertaken in Africa.

Sable Antelope (Swahili: *palahala* or *mbarapi*)

A male sable, with its distinctive sweeping sickle-shaped long
horns, a black satin-like coat and a contrasting white face and belly,
has to be one of the most beautiful of all the large antelope.
Female sable are a rich chestnut in colour and can easily be
confused with roan antelope. Sable antelope were never common
in Kenya and the few that are left all live in the Shimba Hills
National Reserve. Sables are gregarious, living in small groups in
light woodland with clearings. The groups consist of herds of
females with their young, bachelor groups of young males and
solitary dominant males. The dominant male, which becomes

Tana River Primate National Reserve

Tana River Primate National Reserve

Location: 350km (217 miles) from Nairobi, 160km (100 miles) from Malindi.

Size: 169km² (65 sq miles).

Altitude: 40–70m (130–230ft).

Of interest: This reserve has seven species of primate, plus elephant, hippo, lion, waterbuck and crocodile.

Accommodation: *Mchelelo Research Camp* run by Institute of Primate Research, National Museums of Kenya: www.museums.or.ke

A self-catering tented camp: tourism@kws.org

darker and more obvious with age, stands in a prominent spot in his territory waiting for female herds to pass by. His territory, marked by dung piles, is usually the best grazing in the area, so sooner or later a group of females will arrive. The territorial male will try to keep the female herds in his territory, especially if there is a female in oestrus. Young males are also allowed in his territory as long as they are subordinate and show no interest in the females.

Young bulls generally leave the maternal herd when they are about four years old; by then they have become much darker than the females and are constantly harassed by the territorial males. The young males are very vulnerable to predators at this time, until they can join one of the bachelor herds, while young females stay with the maternal herd for the rest of their lives.

Tana River Primate National Reserve

This reserve was created in 1976 to protect two endangered primates: the crested mangabey and the Tana River red colobus. The reserve on the banks of the Tana River is a relic of the Central African lowland rainforest which at one time stretched across the width of Africa and, because of this, much of the flora and fauna is unusual to East Africa. Although a protected area since 1976, at least 50% of the forest was cut down (between 1994 and 2000) by local people, the Pokomo tribe, who thought that their ancestral land was being taken away from them and given to monkeys.

Arawale National Reserve

Location: 130km (81 miles) north of Malindi.

Size: 533km² (206 sq miles).

Altitude: 85–100m (280–328ft).

Of interest: This reserve protects Hunter's hartebeest, plus elephant, hippo, buffalo and crocodile.

In all, seven species of primate occur in the reserve, including blue and black-faced vervet monkeys, olive baboons and three different bushbabies (galagos). Also occurring in the reserve are elephants, Kirk's dikdik, leopard, lion, reticulated giraffe, hippo, common and red duikers, Grant's gazelle, buffalo, both Grevy's and Burchell's zebra, lesser kudu, common waterbuck and, seasonally, the rare and endangered hirola antelope.

Arawale National Reserve

Established in 1974, Arewale has no park entrance and there is no visitor fee. This reserve is a sanctuary for Hunter's hartebeest; also occurring there are buffalo, crocodile, elephant, hippo and lesser kudu.

Marine National Parks and Reserves

Arabuko-Sokoke Forest National Park and Reserve

Located south of Watamu, 6km² (2 sq miles) of this forest has been declared a national park. A remnant of the coastal forest, it was once famous for its indigenous rubber trees (*Milicia excelsa*), avifauna and butterfly population. It is the only place in the country where the rare Ader's duiker and the golden-rumped elephant shrew live. Bird species seen here include the Sokoke Pipit and the Sokoke Scops Owl.

Marine National Parks and Reserves

Mombasa Marine National Park

This park, established in 1986, is 10km² (4 sq miles) in area. It was created to protect the corals and coral fishes. The park is surrounded by a 200km² (77 sq mile) Marine National Reserve, where traditional fishing is allowed under licence.

Kinunga Marine National Reserve

This marine reserve lies some 225km (140 miles) north of Malindi. Here visitors can see the rare dugong and green turtle.

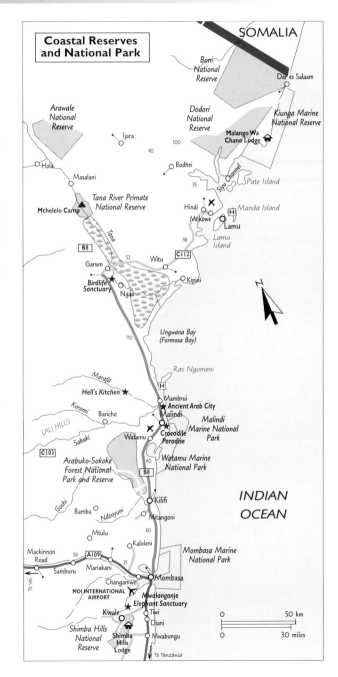

Coastal Reserves and National Park

ROHOLE, KORA AND MERU

This area is 'Born Free' country made famous by George and Joy Adamson. It is real safari country with open savannahs, baobab trees and dense riverine forest along the banks of the two major rivers which flow through the park and along the Tana River, which forms the southern boundary.

After years of neglect and serious poaching, Meru National Park has been reborn. The park has been restocked with wildlife and, once again, is a wonderful place to visit, especially for birders. Birders should look out for Pel's Fishing Owls and Peters' Finfoot along the Rojeweru River, and also the breeding colonies of Madagascar Bee-eaters along the Tana River. Rohole National Reserve, by contrast, is not open to visitors.

Top Ten

Grevy's zebra
Beisa oryx
Reticulated giraffe
Black rhino
White rhino
Pel's Fishing Owl
Peters' Finfoot
Madagascar Bee-eaters
Visit Elsa's grave
Visit Elsa's Camp

Opposite, top to bottom:
The wonderful view from Elsa's Kopje Lodge; a beautiful male reticulated giraffe crosses a road in Meru National Park; a male elephant feeding under an acacia tree in Meru National Park.

Rohole and Kora National Reserves

Rohole National Reserve

Rohole National Reserve

Location: 460km (286 miles) from Nairobi.
Size: 1270km² (490 sq miles).
Altitude: 250–480m (820–1575ft).
Of interest: Dry thorn bush country; wildlife includes elephant, Grevy's zebra and beisa oryx.

Rohole National Reserve lies to the east of Meru National Park. Although at a lower altitude to Meru, like Meru it consists of dry thorn bush country, with the Tana River forming its southern boundary. Elephant, Grevy's zebra and reticulated giraffe occur but there are no visitor facilities. Rohole is being used as an experiment to see how local tribes can coexist with wildlife.

Kora National Reserve

Kora National Reserve consists of inhospitable, dry acacia thorn bush, interspersed with granite kopjes. During 1983 and 1984 a joint expedition of the National Museums of Kenya and the Royal Geographic Society studied this little-known area, which proved to be a remarkable ecosystem virtually untouched by man. The book *Islands in the Bush*, written by the expedition's leader, Malcolm Coe, records their findings. It was in the Kora Reserve that George Adamson, from 1970 onwards, made his final home. Still rehabilitating lions up to the time of his death, George was gunned down and murdered on 20 August 1989 by Somali poachers. For years access to Kora was very difficult and there are few roads. In 1999 KWS built a bridge over the Tana River linking Meru National Park with Kora, making Kora much more accessible.

Kora National Reserve

Location: 410km (255 miles) from Nairobi.
Size: 1737km² (690 sq miles).
Altitude: 250–440m (820–1444ft).
Of interest: This was George Adamson's last home. During the 1980s the area was studied by a joint expedition of the National Museums of Kenya and the Royal Geographical Society. Out of this came *Islands in the Bush* by the expedition leader, Malcolm Coe. No visitor facilities.

Meru National Park

One of Kenya's lesser-known and less-visited wildlife areas, Meru is perhaps best known for Elsa, the lioness that Joy Adamson rehabilitated to the wilds. This story was made famous by the book, written by Joy, and the film *Born Free*, a story about the lives of Joy, her husband George Adamson and Elsa, the lioness they reared from a cub. Joy also reared a cheetah called Pippa here in Meru, which became the subject of another one of Joy's books, *The Spotted Sphinx*. It is possible to visit Pippa's grave site which is in the riverine forest close to the Rojewero River.

Meru National Park was first gazetted in 1966 by the local county council, the first African council to do so. The park is an area of unspoilt wilderness with views of Mount Kenya and, despite its good network of well-maintained roads, instils the feeling of real wild Africa. The park's attraction lies in the diversity of its scenery and its wide variety of habitats, ranging from forest, dry

Meru National Park

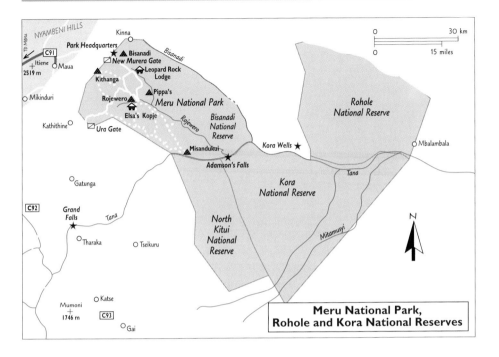

Meru National Park,
Rohole and Kora National Reserves

bush and grasslands to swamps and numerous small permanent rivers lined with doum and raffia palms, tamarind trees and various acacias. The Rojewero River, roughly bisecting the park, is the most beautiful of the rivers. Along its banks bird-watchers should look out for the rarely seen Peters' Finfoot and the unusual Palm-nut Vulture.

The eastern part of the park consists of open grassland plains, while the western part is more wooded. There is also a huge contrast in the rainfall; the western area has almost double that of the east. There are a number of prominent inselbergs, including Mughwango (where George Adamson had a camp) and Leopard Rock. There is now a small luxury lodge (nine cottages) on Mughwango with stunning views of the park.

Meru's wildlife, although not as approachable as in other more visited parks, is varied and often numerous. Lion, leopard and cheetah are usually sighted, as well as elephant and buffalo; hippo

Meru National Park

Location: 370km (230 miles) from Nairobi, via Nanyuki.

Size: 870km^2 (300 sq miles).

Altitude: 366–914m (1200–3000ft).

Of interest: The home of *Born Free*, the book (and film) describing George and Joy Adamson's life rearing a lion cub called Elsa.

Accommodation:

Elsa's Kopje: www.chelipeacock.com

Leopard Rock Lodge: www.leopardmico.com

Meru National Park

Translocated Animals

The total number of animals now translocated to Meru National Park is as follows:

Elephants 66
Grevy's zebra 20
Common zebra 611
Impala 411
White rhino 23
Black rhino 4
Reticulated giraffe 71
Bohor reedbuck 128
Leopard 18

and crocodile are plentiful in the larger rivers. Both Burchell's and the endangered Grevy's zebra occur, as do reticulated giraffe, gerenuk, Grant's gazelle, and both greater and lesser kudu. Over 400 species of birds have been recorded, including Pel's Fishing Owl and African Finfoot.

In the 1980s the park was hit by Somali poachers. Its large elephant herds (more than 3000) were decimated and a herd of white rhino that had been introduced from South Africa were all shot, along with their carers. But Meru is now recovering; during the last few years Meru, with the help of generous donations from Europe, has been rehabilitated. Black rhino and reticulated giraffe have been reintroduced and the road network repaired. Recently IFAW (International Fund for Animal Welfare), in partnership with the KWS and Dr Richard Leakey, committed to a five-year plan costing US$1.25 million. Very soon 66 elephants were translocated from private ranches in Laikipia. These elephants were captured as family groups and moved one at a time to ensure they stayed together. Next, four black rhinos and 20 Grevy's zebra were moved to Meru. In 2002 the Agence Francaise de Developpement (AFD) gave a grant of US$ 7 million; part of this fund is to be used in Meru's rehabilitation.

White rhino (Swahili: *kifaru*)

White rhino are the second largest (in size – hippo weigh more) mammal after the elephant. Males weigh 2040–2260kg (4497–4982lb) and females average 1600kg (3527lb), almost twice the bulk of a black rhino; they have a pronounced hump and a wide, square mouth. White rhino are not white, except at Lake Nakuru National Park, where they take up the colour of the white soda. It is thought they get their name from the Afrikaans word *wyd* (wide), for their wide mouths. White rhino are grazers, using their square mouths to feed efficiently on short grass.

Mature bulls are usually solitary except when they join a female in oestrus. Females have overlapping territories and are generally accompanied by their recent offspring. Juveniles leave their mother at about two to three years old, usually when their mother has calved again. These juveniles often join up together

White rhino

and may temporarily join up with a female without a calf. Larger groups of up to 12 white rhino do occur, mostly during the midday heat, when they lie together in a shady, breezy place.

Baobab tree (Swahili: *mbuyu*)

The baobab is focal to many African legends and superstitions and is revered. With its 'upside-down' look, the baobab looks like a squat prehistoric monster. Legend has it that God, in a fit of anger because the baobab tree could not decide which habitat it required, threw the tree over his shoulder. It landed on its crown and has grown roots upwards ever since. Its grotesquely swollen bottle-shaped trunk and smooth grey bark store water, allowing the baobab to survive in drought conditions. Its thick branches, which look more like roots, are devoid of leaves for much of the year.

Baobabs are among the longest living trees in the world; carbon dating has shown that trees 5m (15ft) in diameter may be 1000 years old. Larger ones may be as old as 3000 years. Portuguese

Below: A white rhino drinking at a water hole; its 'wide' mouth, from which it gets its name, is clearly seen.

Meru National Park

*Right: A rare Pel's Fishing Owl.
These owls occur in Meru
National Park.*

cannonballs from four centuries ago have been found in living trees that line the approach to Mombasa harbour. Many of the older trees are more than 5–7m (15–20ft) in diameter.

This is a very useful tree: its trunk, which is often hollow, holds water for wildlife; its flowers are pollinated by bats and bushbabies, and its fibres are twisted into ropes. Its fruit contains tartaric acid and is high in vitamin C; its pulp, soaked in water, makes a very refreshing drink. During droughts elephants gouge out the trunks with their tusks and eat the moist fibre, causing many trees to collapse. Surprisingly, many survive the elephants' onslaught and continue to grow, even with large holes in them. Baobabs are found in many parts of eastern Kenya below 1300m (4000ft).

Pel's Fishing Owl

This owl is very uncommon in Kenya but it is resident along the Rojewero River in the Meru National Park. They are probably more common than records suggest but unfortunately these owls are very difficult to see as they roost in large shady trees

Doum Palm

overhanging the water. When they are seen, it is usually because they have been disturbed and the only view of them is as they fly away. Pel's Fishing Owls are large (64–76cm/25–30in), rufous-coloured owls which hunt their prey, fish, in shallow water from a low branch or the river bank.

Doum palm (Swahili: *mkoma*)

This distinctive palm, the only one with a divided trunk, is found along river courses throughout eastern Kenya, particularly in hot, dry areas. Its orange fruit, 8–10cm (3–4in) when ripe, is eaten by the local people. Baboons and elephant also eat them. It's not uncommon to see a troop of baboons feeding on the fruit high in the tree with a group of elephant feeding on any that are dropped by the baboons. In fact, it is thought that the fruit has to pass through the gut of an elephant before it can germinate. The nut, called vegetable ivory, is carved and necklaces and buttons are made from it. The leaves are woven into baskets and mats and the Turkana people use the leaves for building their huts. The sap is used to make a strong alcoholic drink.

Below: A herd of endangered Grevy's zebras grazing below a doum palm.

SIBILOI, CENTRAL ISLAND, SOUTH ISLAND, SAIWA SWAMP AND MOUNT ELGON

L ake Turkana and the Sibiloi National Park are often referred to as the 'The Cradle of Mankind.' This is where the Leakey family have researched for many years. The archaeological site at Koobi Fora is well worth a visit, although visitors must either fly there by charter aircraft or tackle some of the worse road/tracks in Africa, including crossing the Chalbi desert. Visitors must be self-sufficient.

Saiwa Swamp National Park is Kenya's smallest national park. This tiny national park is a great place to see the rare sitatunga antelope and spotted-necked otters, which can be viewed from walkways over the swamp and from tree platforms. Mount Elgon National Park, by contrast, is a forest-covered mountain with deep caves into which elephants and other wildlife enter, in search of essential minerals.

Top Ten

Sitatunga (Saiwa Swamp NP)

Spotted-necked otter (Saiwa Swamp NP)

Giant forest squirrel (Saiwa Swamp NP)

Tiang (Sibiloi NP)

Crocodiles (Central Island NP)

Northern Carmine Bee-eaters (Sibiloi NP)

Heuglin's Bustard (Sibiloi NP)

Arabian Bustard (Sibiloi NP)

Colobus monkeys (Mount Elgon NP)

Giant forest hogs (Mount Elgon NP)

Opposite, top to bottom: A doum palm on the shore of the Jade Sea (Lake Turkana); a view of Saiwa Swamp from one of the tree platforms; an El Molo village at Lake Turkana.

Sibiloi National Park

Sibiloi National Park

Location: 720km (450 miles) from Nairobi.

Size: 1570km² (600 sq miles).

Altitude: 200m (650ft).

Of interest: Koobi Fora, where Dr Richard Leakey's team has discovered fossils representing one of man's earliest ancestors.

Accommodation: Visitors may stay overnight at Koobi Fora. The accommodation consists of a number of bandas, but visitors must be self-sufficient. Book through National Museums, www.museums.or.ke

Sibiloi National Park

Sibiloi National Park, situated on the eastern shore of Lake Turkana (also called the Jade Sea because of its unusual blue-green colour which changes as the winds and light change), was gazetted in 1968 to protect the sites of early hominid fossil finds by Richard Leakey's team. Some of their discoveries date back from between 3 million and 1 million years ago. There is a small museum near the park headquarters with exhibits of some of the finds, including part of a 1.5-million-year-old elephant. The national park also includes Central Island, which is formed out of three dormant volcanoes, the highest one reaching to 240m (800ft). The climate is hot; the average temperature throughout the year is 40°C (104°F) and windy. The terrain consists of volcanic rock, desert and dry bush. Vegetation is sparse, with yellow spear grass and doum palms. The almost ceaseless winds in the area have exposed many of the fossil finds.

Sibiloi National Park has a surprising amount and variety of wildlife, despite its being extremely arid and windblown. It includes lion, cheetah, Grevy's zebra, beisa oryx, gerenuk, Grant's gazelle and a unique family member of the topi, called the tiang.

Bird life, too, is varied and at times plentiful, especially during the European winter months, when the lake shore is home to large numbers of wading birds, among them Black-tailed Godwits and Redshanks. For the really keen bird-watcher, the birds found in the arid bush are perhaps the most interesting: Swallow-tailed Kites, Heuglin's and Kori Bustards, Lichtenstein's Sandgrouse, Somali and Carmine Bee-eaters, and both Crested and Short-crested Larks are just a few of the wonderful birds found here.

Koobi Fora

Koobi Fora, on the eastern shore of Lake Turkana, is the headquarters of Sibiloi National Park. The area is virtually uninhabited except for the nomadic Gabbra people. Here is a small museum where some of the Leakey team's archaeological finds are displayed. The area has yielded large numbers of fossils representing both australopithecines and early hominids, including a skull of *Homo habilis* (KNM-ER 1470), one of the earliest recognized species of man, discovered by Dr Richard Leakey.

Sibiloi National Park

It is also here that hominid fossils confirmed that man stood upright more than 4 million years ago.

Even though the area is hot – it can reach 46°C (115°F) – and inhospitable, with almost incessant winds, for anyone interested in archaeology it is a fascinating place to visit. On a walk around the area even individuals with untrained eyes can easily see fossils lying on the surface. It is possible to stay overnight here, but visitors must be fully equipped. A fee of 500 Kenya Shillings per person is charged.

Tiang (Swahili: *nyamera*)

Tiang are close relatives of topi but live in more arid country. The best place to see them is Koobi Fora on the eastern shore of Lake Turkana.

Lichtenstein's Sandgrouse

Sandgrouse live in hot, dry, open country where they feed mostly on seeds. These areas are usually far from water. Each morning or evening, depending on the species, large flocks, sometimes thousands strong, fly up to 80km (50 miles) from their feeding or breeding areas to water holes to drink. The sight and sound of thousands of sandgrouse arriving at and leaving a water hole is an amazing experience. On arrival they circle the water hole, land and then quickly run down to the water's edge where they line up, taking several quick sips of water before flying off in a whirl of wings. Male sandgrouse have a special duty to perform while drinking. If the sandgrouse have chicks, the male, who has

Map

Todenyang, C47, LAPURR RANGE, Lokitaung, 45, MURUA RITH HILLS, Lake Turkana, North Island, Koobi Fora, KALIMAPUS HILLS, Ferguson's Gulf, Fishing Spot, Kalokol, Lake Turkana Fishing Lodge, A1, Kalokol, 58, A1, Eliye Springs, Eliye Springs Fishing Lodge, 48, Lodwar, Turkwel, Tolkoruma, 83, Lokichar, KAMUTILE HILLS, A1, KATIGITHIGIRIA HILLS

SUDAN, Lake Chew Bahir (Lake Stefanie), Olleret, Sabarei, Jibisa, 1543 m, Crocodile Sanctuary, Sibiloi National Park, Lishode Peak, PUCKOON RIDGE, Derati, Allia Bay, Central Island, Central Island NP, Gajos, North Horr, To Marsabit, El Molo, C77, Oasis Lodge, Mt Kulal, Loiyangalani, El Molo 2295 m, South Island NP, Kibrot Pass, South Island, NACHORUGWAI DESERT, Kerio, N, 0 — 50 km, 0 — 30 miles, 85, Lokichar, To Kitale, Loperot

Sibiloi, South Island and Central Island National Parks

Sibiloi National Park

Central Island National Park

Location: 760km (472 miles) from Nairobi, via Lodwar, to Kolokol, then a boat ride.
Size: 5km² (2 sq miles).
Altitude: 460m (1500ft).
Of interest: One of Africa's largest populations of crocodiles, which breed in the three lakes on the island.

special belly feathers that can absorb water, crouches down low in the water, thoroughly soaking the belly feathers before setting off on its long flight back to its nest. On arrival at the nest he fluffs out his feathers and the chicks drink from them. Strangely, the female does not have this adaptation. Lichtenstein's Sandgrouse live in the arid, stony areas of northern Kenya and mostly fly to water holes to drink after sunset or before dawn.

Central Island National Park

Central Island lies 15km (9 miles) from the nearest shore of Lake Turkana. The island is formed out of three still steaming volcanoes, the highest 250m (800ft) tall. Each volcano is filled with a lake and each is a different colour; one has a large population of crocodiles, while another is usually fringed with flamingo. There are also a number of boiling geysers on the island.

South Island National Park

South Island is the tip of a volcano lying 6.5km (4 miles) from Lake Turkana's eastern shore and 24km (15 miles) from the southern shore. The island is covered by volcanic ash and at night a ghostly glow from its luminous vents may well be the reason the local people, the El Molo (Kenya's smallest tribe, numbering only a few hundred people), think that the island is a place of ill omen and never visit there. There is no wildlife on the island apart from a small herd of feral goats.

The first known person to visit South Island was the explorer Sir Vivian Fuchs (of Antarctica fame) who landed there in 1934 accompanied by his expedition's surveyor, Snaffles Martin. Fuchs returned to the mainland and sent the team's doctor, Bill Dyson, to join Martin. Fuchs had arranged that Martin and Dyson would send smoke signals every day. After a few days the signals stopped and when Fuchs returned to the island he found no trace of them; neither Martin or Dyson nor their boat was ever seen again. The waters of Lake Turkana are regularly whipped up by 100kph (60mph) winds, which turn the lake into a tempest.

Saiwa Swamp National Park

Saiwa Swamp National Park, Kenya's and Africa's smallest, was created to protect a population of sitatunga antelope. The park

Saiwa Swamp National Park

consists of a long, narrow, swampy valley filled with rushes and sedges, bordered by a narrow band of riverine forest. This is an ideal habitat for the sitatunga, which has evolved specially adapted hooves to live in this swampy environment. A good feature of the park is that there are no roads, so visitors have to do all their viewing of animals and birds on foot. Over the swamp there are wooden walkways leading to several observation towers. The towers have been built along the edge of the swamp to enable visitors to view the sitatunga and other wildlife. From the towers, if one stays quiet and still, it is also possible to see the rare De Brazza monkey as well as Sykes' and colobus monkeys. Other wildlife in this tiny sanctuary are olive baboons, bushbuck, reedbuck, suni, giant forest squirrels and spotted-necked otters.

Sitatunga (Swahili: _nzohe_)
Sitatunga are large aquatic-dwelling antelope, 100–120cm (45–50in) at the shoulder and weighing 45–110kg (100–240lb). Males are larger than females and different in colour, and have spiral horns about 36cm (25in) long. Sitatunga have a shaggy coat which is well adapted to its aquatic environment. The males are greyish-brown in colour while the females are a rich chocolate brown. On the body there are faint white vertical stripes, which are not always readily seen, and there is a prominent white

South Island National Park

Location: 590km (367 miles) from Nairobi, via Maralal, to Loiyangalani, then a boat ride.
Size: 39km² (15 sq miles).
Altitude: 460m (1500ft).
Of interest: This is the scene of a mysterious tragedy involving an expedition led by Vivian Fuchs. Two members of his expedition disappeared from this island.

Saiwa Swamp National Park

Location: 20km (12 miles) from Kitale.
Size: 2km² (0.8 sq miles).
Altitude: 1860–1880m (6135ft).
Of interest: The population of sitatunga which live in this tiny national park.

Left: A male sitatunga feeding in Saiwa Swamp National Park. The sitatunga can be observed from tree platforms which give wonderful views.

Mount Elgon National Park

Mount Elgon National Park

Location: 400km (250 miles) from Nairobi.

Size: 169km² (65 sq miles).

Altitude: 2336–4321m (7664–14,177ft).

Of interest: The lava caves attract elephants, which enter them at night in search of salts.

Accommodation: KWS Bandas: www.kws.org
Nearby Lokitela Farm, bookings through Bush and Beyond: www.bush-and-beyond.com

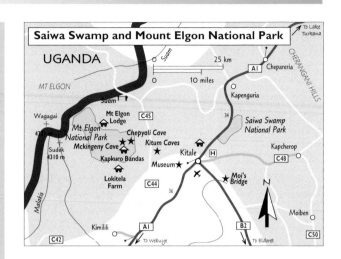

Saiwa Swamp and Mount Elgon National Park

chevron between the eyes. The sitatunga's feet are most remarkable; the hooves are long and splayed, which allows them to walk on soft ground and floating vegetation. Sitatunga are both browsers and grazers, spending their day deep in a swamp, sometimes partially submerged, as they feed on sedges, leaves and grass. At night they often leave the swamp to graze on grasses along the edge of the swamp. They are mostly solitary except at times of mating. The gestation period is about 7½ months and after birth the calf is left 'lying out' (see panel, page 83) for about a month. During 1990 and 1991, with the permission of the Kenya Wildlife Service, 10 sitatunga were released into a swamp at Lewa Downs. This population is now well established and is increasing in numbers.

Mount Elgon National Park

For miles around, Mount Elgon dominates the skyline; it is Kenya's second highest mountain. Part of the mountain, which is actually an extinct caldera, is a national park, one of the most scenic and unspoilt in Kenya. Mount Elgon sits astride the Kenya/Uganda border and is known to the Maasai who once lived in the area as Ol Doinyo Igoon which translates as 'Mountain of the breast'. The highest peak is Wagagai, at 4321m (14,176ft). It is actually in Uganda but climbers are allowed to climb it from the Kenya side of the border. The volcano's caldera is 6–8km (4–5

Mount Elgon National Park

miles) across. The park, founded in 1949, lies on the eastern flank of this volcanic mountain. Elgon's lower slopes are forest-covered, containing some of Kenya's finest *Podocarpus* sp. trees, which slowly give way to beautiful afro-alpine moorlands with giant heaths and giant groundsel. The crater floor, at an altitude of 3500m (11,480ft), comprises a luxuriant groundsel forest and has a number of hot springs which form the source of the Suam River. One of Elgon's special features is that hiking and trout fishing are permitted in the national park.

Mount Elgon also has a number of lava tube caves, some several hundred feet deep. Three are accessible, these being Kitum, Chepyali and Mackingeny. Although the latter cave is the most spectacular, Kitum is the best known as it formed the subject of a wildlife film. The caves and the elephants have been the subject of much research and have been made into a wildlife documentary by the BBC. Mountain vegetation lacks certain minerals which are essential to the health of all wildlife. Because of the lack of certain minerals, local elephants have for hundreds and perhaps thousands of years visited Mount Elgon's caves, particularly Kitum, to gouge into them, sometimes for quite long distances, in their constant search for essential mineral salts. Other mammals, such as buffalo, bushbuck and duiker, also require theses minerals and have followed the elephants' path into the caves. Apparently Mount Elgon's Kitum Cave inspired Rider Haggard's book, *She*.

Left: *Looking down into Uganda from Mount Elgon.*

MARSABIT, LOSAI, SHABA, SAMBURU, BUFFALO SPRINGS AND LAIKIPIA REGION

The Northern Frontier District, Buffalo Springs, Samburu and Shaba Reserves are a must-visit for wildlife enthusiasts. The wildlife here is so different from elsewhere in Africa. Grevy's zebra, reticulated giraffe, beisa oryx, gerenuk and Somali Ostrich are all common here. Cheetah, lion, and leopard are also regularly sighted. Special birds for the birding enthusiasts are Somali Bee-eater, Somali Courser, Vulturine Guineafowl and the stunning Golden-breasted Starlings.

Marsabit National Reserve is a forest-covered mountain which rises out of a desert and was the home of Ahmed, a huge elephant with big tusks, who was protected by presidential decree. Marsabit is still the home of many elephants and some special birds. Losai National Reserve is, by contrast, a lava plateau, with a number of volcanic cones. This area is virtually inaccessible, even by 4WD vehicles, but there is an airstrip which serves a mission station, Ngoronet.

Top Ten

Gerenuk

Beisa oryx

Reticulated giraffe

Grevy's zebra

Greater kudu

Leopard

Vulturine Guineafowl

Somali Bee-eater

Somali Courser

Somali Ostrich

Opposite, top to bottom: A herd of Grevy's zebra in Shaba National Reserve; a family of dwarf mongooses on the alert; a beisa oryx drinking in the Ewaso Ngiro River in the Samburu National Reserve.

Marsabit National Reserve

Marsabit National Reserve

Location: 560km (348 miles) from Nairobi.

Size: 1500km² (579 sq miles).

Altitude: 420–1675m (1378–5495ft).

Of interest: Marsabit National Reserve is the place where American film-makers Martin and Olsa Johnson produced some of the earliest wildlife films in the 1920s.

Accommodation: Marsabit Lodge: tel: +254 69 2411.

Marsabit National Reserve

Marsabit is a forested mountain, with spectacular volcanic craters, which rises out of the Chalbi Desert. It was first made famous by the American film-makers Martin and Olsa Johnson, who lived there for four years in the 1920s and made some of the first wildlife films. Later Marsabit became known as the home of Ahmed, a huge tusked bull elephant, who was protected by presidential decree. President Jomo Kenyatta declared Ahmed a national monument, granting him presidential protection until his death. Ahmed died as the result of old age in 1974. Ahmed's body has been preserved and is on display at the National Museum, Nairobi.

Greater Kudu (Swahili: *tandala mkubwa*)

The most striking of all the antelopes, the males have long, spectacular spiralled horns which can grow as long as 180cm (7in), forming at least 2½ graceful twists. These beautifully shaped horns have long been prized by hunters and in African culture for use as a musical horn and symbolic ritual object. In some cultures the horns are thought to be the dwelling place of powerful spirits, and in others they are a symbol of male potency. Such long horns should be a hindrance in the wooded habitat where these animals live. But the kudu just tilts back its head and, with its horns lying along its back, walks and even runs easily through dense bush.

Like their relatives, the eland, greater kudu can make spectacular leaps of up to 2.5m (6ft). Greater kudus are tall; males average 135cm (54in) at the shoulder and weigh about 257kg (565lb). Females, as tall but without horns, are noticeably more slender, weighing on average 170kg (374lb).

Greater kudu are browsers living in dry bush areas but in dry seasons they will eat wild melons, other fruits and even Sodom apple and aloes. Females form small herds of 6–10 individuals and are only joined by a male in the mating season. Male kudu are usually solitary, but sometimes form into small bachelor groups. After a gestation period of 7–8 months the females leave the herd to give birth. After birth the female leaves the young calf 'lying out' (see panel, page 83) for four to five weeks, one of the longest periods of all the antelope family; the calf is three or four months old before its mother rejoins its herd.

Losai National Reserve

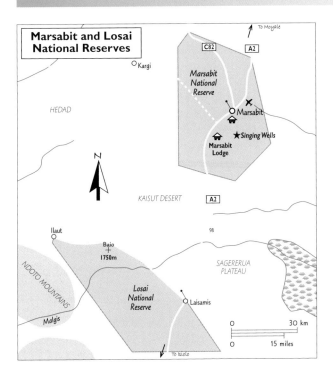

Marsabit and Losai National Reserves

Somali Ostrich (Swahili: *mbuni*)

Somali Ostrich occur in the northeastern dry bush country. Males differ from the Common Ostrich in that their neck and legs are blue. During the breeding season the blue brightens and the bill and the front of the legs become bright pink.

Ostrich have an unusual breeding system, with one major female and five or six minor females laying, on average, 25 eggs in the nest. The eggs are usually incubated by the major female during the day and the male at night. The chicks leave the nest three or four days after hatching and join up with other chicks in the area, forming a crèche which sometimes numbers more than 100. The crèches are looked after by only one adult pair.

Losai National Reserve

This reserve was established in 1976 to protect the habitat and its wildlife. There are no visitor facilities.

Losai National Reserve

Location: 368km (229 miles) north of Nairobi.

Size: 1806km² (697 sq miles).

Altitude: 625–1750m (2050–5740ft).

Of interest: Closed to tourism, Kenya's least-known game sanctuary is located in the Kiasut Desert. The reserve consists of a lava plateau dissected by dry luggas.

Shaba National Reserve

Shaba National Reserve

Shaba National Reserve

Location: 325km (202 miles) from Nairobi.

Size: 239km² (92 sq miles).

Altitude: 700–1500m (2300–4920ft).

Of interest: This is the place where the late Joy Adamson lived while she reared a leopard cub. The reserve is scenically stunning.

Accommodation:

Joy Adamson's Camp (ten tents): www.chelipeacock.com

Sarova Shaba: www.sarovahotels.com

Although Shaba, lying to the east of the Samburu and Buffalo Springs reserves, is only separated from them by a major highway, it is a very different habitat. It is scenically dramatic; here the Ewaso Ngiro, which forms the reserve's northern boundary for 34km (20 miles), instead of coursing through a plain, runs through deep gorges and waterfalls. Mount Bodech and Shaba Hill dominate the landscape, and the plains are dotted with springs, small swamps and rocky hills. The wildlife is similar to that of the other reserves but generally not as plentiful or as tame.

Shaba is perhaps best known as the one-time home of author Joy Adamson who rehabilitated a leopard called Penny here. The story is told in Joy's book, *Penny, Queen of Shaba*. It was at Shaba that Joy was murdered.

Samburu and Buffalo Springs National Reserves

These two small scenic reserves range in altitude from 800–1230m (2625–4036ft). They sit astride the Ewaso Ngiro River (a Samburu word meaning 'river of brown water') and are dominated by the impressive sheer-walled Ol Lolokwe and the

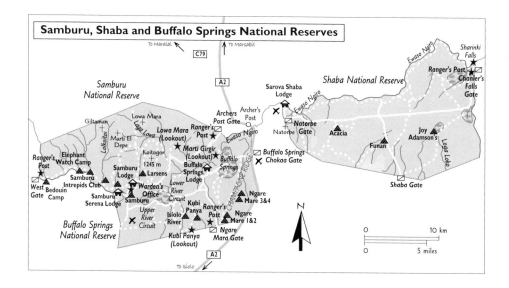

Samburu and Buffalo Springs National Reserves

rocky hills of Koitogor and Lolkoitoi. The river, bordered by a green ribbon of riverine forest made up mostly of tamarind trees, doum palms, Tana River poplars, and the *Acacia elatior*, is the lifeblood of this dry, arid region.

In the Samburu National Reserve north of the river, a narrow plain quickly gives way to rocky hillsides which are home to many leopards, while Buffalo Springs National Reserve is mainly a rolling plain of volcanic soils with dry river beds lined with doum palms.

Buffalo Springs Reserve has two small but important rivers flowing through it: the Isiolo River, which never dries up (the Ewaso Ngiro occasionally does), and the Ngare Mara. There are also the crystal-clear springs which give the reserve its name. Unfortunately, their beauty has been spoilt: one of the springs has had an unsightly wall built around it and its water piped to the nearby small town of Archer's Post, while another has a smaller wall around it and is used as a swimming pool for campers. Fortunately, one small spring has been left in its natural state and its waters flow into the nearby Ewaso Ngiro River, providing a magnet for wildlife.

Near Buffalo Springs is a wonderful area called Champagne Ridge, covered with flat-topped Umbrella Thorn Trees (*Acacia tortilis*), which are characteristic of the area. On either side of the river are extensive areas of Salt Bush (*Salsola dendroides*), which few animals eat because its leaves taste salty, but it does provide cover for lion and cheetah.

It is the unique wildlife that attracts many tourists to this wonderful area and, although there are no large spectacular herds to see, there is a wide variety. Four very special mammals – gerenuk, Grevy's zebra, beisa oryx and reticulated giraffe – are all quite common here and, although there is some seasonal movement out of the reserves, you can usually count on seeing them when you visit here. Other mammals include Burchell's zebra, buffalo, impala, common waterbuck, dikdik (both Kirk's and Gunther's), Grant's gazelle, klipspringer, both greater and lesser kudu and warthog.

Samburu and Buffalo Springs National Reserves

Location: 325km (202 miles) from Nairobi.

Size (Samburu): 104km² (40 sq miles).

Size (Buffalo Springs): 194km² (75 sq miles).

Altitude: 800–1230m (2625–4036ft).

Of interest: Maralal Donkey Safaris in Samburuland, e-mail: info@samburutrails.com www.samburutrails.com

Accommodation: *see panel, page 78.*

Private Reserves in the Laikipia region

The highlight of any visit to Samburu and Buffalo Springs is to watch the large numbers of elephant (unperturbed by safari-goers) drinking and bathing in the shallow waters of the Ewaso Ngiro River. Crocodiles and the occasional hippo are present in the river, although it is not an ideal environment for hippos as the dry bush to either side of the river provides them with very little food.

Private Reserves in the Laikipia region

The Laikipia ecosystem covers 809,389ha (2 million acres). Located northwest of Mount Kenya, Laikipia is a sparsely populated area, much of it covered by large, privately owned ranches that include a wide range of landscapes from high plains to forested valleys. On some ranches cattle and sheep share the land with the wildlife. Some are sanctuaries created by the local communities, which have combined small farms and grazing land into large group ranches. (For more information, visit www.laikipia.org)

Lewa Wildlife Conservancy

A member of the Laikipia Wildlife Forum, Lewa Downs, now called the Lewa Wildlife Conservancy, is owned by the Craig family. Originally a cattle ranch where wildlife was encouraged, it now has an amazing variety of wildlife, ranging from elephant and rhino to leopard and dikdik. The wildlife has done so well that, in the case of the reticulated giraffe, it has sometimes done too well. Their numbers increased so much that they were damaging the environment, so several of them were successfully translocated to other wildlife areas including Meru National Park.

It is at Lewa that Anna Mertz, with the help of the Craigs, established the Ngare Sergoi Rhino Sanctuary. Protecting both black and white rhino, it was surrounded by an expensive solar-powered electric fence and patrolled by armed rangers equipped with radios. Later the fence was extended to encircle the entire ranch area, a total distance of 35km (22 miles), and Lewa Downs was renamed. There are now 52 black and 37 white rhino in the conservancy, the figure rising as the population slowly increases. Wildlife that can be seen there include greater kudu, reticulated giraffe, eland, Jackson's hartebeest, both Grevy's and common zebra, gerenuk, impala, Grant's gazelle, bushbuck and buffalo. Among Lewa's attractions are a number of hides (blinds) situated

Borana Ranch

in a swamp, from where it is possible to view the rare sitatunga antelope and many swamp birds. The introduced sitatunga (see page 69) have become more accustomed to visitors and occasionally they can be found feeding in the open on the edge of the swamp. Yet another attraction of a stay at Lewa is being able to walk or ride on horseback among the wildlife. It is also one of the few places in Kenya where guests can take night drives, something that is not allowed in most of Kenya's wildlife areas.

Borana Ranch

Borana is a 14,000ha (35,000-acre) ranch located at an altitude of 2000m (6500ft). Wildlife occurring there includes greater kudu, klipspringer, elephant, buffalo, lion, leopard, cheetah and a variety of antelope. While staying at Borana it is possible to visit the nearby Lewa Wildlife Conservancy to view the rhinos. Other activities are night drives, walks with the local people, and both horse and camel riding. The accommodation is stunning. Borana Lodge has six luxury cottages, each one different, perched on the edge of an escarpment. The view from them is fantastic, with Mount Kenya in the distance and elephants drinking and bathing in a dam below, and also, occasionally, greater kudu drinking. There is also a swimming pool.

Lewa Wildlife Conservancy

Location: 225km (140 miles) from Nairobi.
Size: 9500km² (3667 sq miles).
Altitude: 1615–2896m (5300–9500ft).
Of interest: Both black and white rhino, the rare sitatunga antelope, and greater kudu. Horse riding, hides (blinds) in a swamp.
Accommodation:
Lewa Safari Camp (12 tents):
www.lewa.org
Lewa Wilderness:
www.bush-and-beyond.com

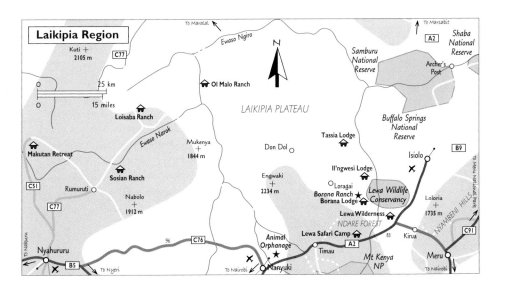

Private Reserves in the Laikipia region

Ol Malo Ranch

Although only 2000ha (5000 acres), Ol Malo is a magic place to visit. It is owned and run by Colin and Rock Francome; an added bonus during your stay here is to talk to the Francomes by an open fire before and during dinner. While the usual drives are available, both day and night, a walk with Colin and one of his staff will remain a highlight of your safari. Also available are camel treks with overnight camping along the Ewaso Ngiro River. Wildlife is varied, with elephants, reticulated giraffe and greater kudu being the main attraction. 'Ol Malo' means 'place of the greater kudu' in the local language. Accommodation is in four beautiful cottages with dramatic views. There is also a swimming pool.

Loisaba Ranch

This 14,000ha (35,000-acre) ranch is located on the edge of the Laikipia plateau. Both day and night drives are available, plus walking, horseback and camel riding. Accommodation comprises seven beautiful cottages, each with a private veranda. There is also a swimming pool and a tennis court at the lodge. Also on the ranch are 'Star Beds' – two rather unusual bush lodges with a difference. One, Kiboko, is set among kopjes and overlooks the Kiboko water hole, while the other, Koija, overlooks the Ewaso Ngiro River. Both are accessible only by camel, horseback or on foot; guests are guided by a team of traditional Samburu and Laikipia Maasai warriors to the sites. At Koija Star Beds, guests cross over the Ewaso Ngiro River on a suspended walkway to the lodge. Both Kiboko and Koija Star Beds comprise two double sleeping platforms and one twin platform. Each double platform is designed for one or two guests. A family platform accommodates four guests sharing bathroom facilities. At Koija two sets of platforms overlook the river and the other has views over a water hole. Each platform is reached by a ladder and has a large double bed, toilet and a camp-style shower with hot and cold water. A thatched roof only partially covers the platform and the beds are on wheels, looking a little like horse-drawn carts, and can be pushed under the thatch if necessary. Normally the beds, which have four-poster insect netting, are left out under the open sky. Each platform is sited to ensure complete privacy. After a wonderful three-course dinner (prepared by specially trained Samburu people) in a thatched dining area, guests retire to their

Sabuk and Ol Ari Nyiro Ranch

star beds. To lie in one of these beds, cosily tucked up against the night chill, listening to the night sounds and looking up at a vista of stars in a clear night sky is a very special experience, and one that you will remember for a long time.

Sabuk

Sabuk is a remote and wonderful wildlife area with a wide variety of animals: greater kudu, elephant, reticulated giraffe, eland and various gazelle can all be seen here. Lion, leopard and cheetah also occur. Sabuk has been conducting camel safaris along the Ewaso Ngiro River for 20 years.

While staying at Sabuk you will be personally hosted by one of the owners, Verity Williams, who has a wealth of experience on safari. Apart from drives, guests can take bush breakfasts and evening sundowners in a wild spot in the area while watching elephants come to drink. Half- or full-day walks or camel treks with local Laikipia Maasai guides can also be arranged. The accommodation comprises five spacious stone cottages, each with a private veranda with stunning views overlooking the Ewaso Ngiro River.

Below: A black rhino browsing on an acacia bush in the Lewa Wildlife Conservancy. This photograph illustrates well the black rhino's pointed lips, in contrast to the wide, square lips of a white rhino.

Ol Ari Nyiro Ranch

This ranch is owned by Kuki Gallmann, the author of *I Dreamed of Africa*. The bush here is rather thick, making wildlife viewing a little more difficult. The real attraction of staying here is the chance of spending some time with Kuki herself; unfortunately though, Kuki cannot guarantee being there during your visit. Guests stay at her home, Makutan Retreat, in three stone-and-thatch cottages, which are built on the edge of the Rift Valley with stunning views of Lakes Bogoria and Baringo.

Grevy's zebra

Il'ngwesi

The Il'ngwesi conservation area is situated next to Lewa Wildlife Conservancy at a lower altitude. The conservation area was created by the local Samburu people with the help of Lewa Wildlife Conservancy. Wildlife in the area includes beisa oryx, reticulated giraffe, Grevy's zebra, gerenuk and dikdik. The Lodge, built by the local people, has six cottages and a swimming pool.

Tassia

Tassia is another conservation area set up by the local people. Visits to the local Samburu people and drives are the main activities here. The Lodge, built by the local people, has six cottages and a swimming pool.

Grevy's zebra (Swahili: *punda milia*)

Grevy's zebra once ranged widely in Ethiopia, Somalia and northern Kenya but now almost all are restricted to parts of northern Kenya. Although they are adapted to semi-arid conditions and require less water than common zebra, they often come into conflict with the nomadic tribes and their livestock (mainly at water points). The Grevy's zebra gets its name from Jules Grevy, president of France in the 1880s, who received one as a gift from Abyssinia. Romans trained them to pull carts in circuses and called them 'hippotigris'.

The Grevy's zebra is taller and larger than the common zebra and its stripes are much narrower and do not reach the belly. Its head is also much bigger and it has very distinctive large rounded ears. Their social behaviour also differs from that of other zebra: Grevy's do not form into large groups and do not migrate in large herds. The adult stallions occupy a territory which they patrol constantly and mark with dung heaps while loudly braying. This distinctive loud braying is a feature that anyone camping near to a stallion's territory will never forget! Loose groups of mares with their young pass through these territories without a problem, but any mare in oestrus can cause fights between males of adjoining territories on their borders. These fights stop the moment the female enters a stallion's territory. Surprisingly, even small bachelor herds are allowed to pass through a stallion's territory if they act submissively.

Gerenuk

Groups of Grevy's zebra appear to have no leaders and, apart from mares with their foals, there are apparently no bonds. Gestation is a little longer than in common zebra – 13 months as against 12 months for a common zebra. Grevy's zebra foals suckle for nine months (common zebra six months) and stay longer with their mothers, so mares usually give birth only once every two years, while the common zebra mares give birth once a year. Grevy's zebra and common zebra occasionally form mixed herds but do not interbreed in the wild. In fact, some researchers consider Grevy's zebra to be more closely related to horses and only called zebras because of their stripes. Grevy's stallions have been bred with horses to produce 'zebroids', but the offspring are sterile.

Gerenuk (Swahili: *swara twiga*)

These elegant, tall, thin, distinctive-looking antelope are common and confiding in the Samburu/Buffalo Springs reserves. Gerenuk is actually the Somali name for these antelopes. They have adapted to feeding at a higher level than other antelopes. They stand erect on their hind legs, with their long necks extended, browsing on leaves out of reach of other similar antelopes. They also use their forelegs to pull down higher branches as high as 1.75–2.5m (6–8ft) off the ground. A gerenuk's head is small, with very large ears; its muzzle is narrow, allowing it to feed carefully between the thorns of acacia trees. It also has flexible upper lips and a long tongue, long eyelashes and sensory hairs on the muzzle and ears to protect the eyes from scratches.

Gerenuk do not require water and get all the moisture they need from the food they eat. Only the males of the species have horns, which are stout, S-shaped and heavily ringed. Both sexes have preorbital glands in front of their eyes which emit a tar-like substance. The males deposit this substance on twigs and bushes to mark their territories. They also have scent glands on their knees and between their split hooves.

Gerenuk live in small groups (2–8) of related females and their young, or bachelor groups or as solitary males. They are found in dry bush country in northern and eastern Kenya below 1220m (4000ft) and apparently were only discovered as a species in 1878.

Antelope 'lying out'

Most female antelope leave the herd to give birth. After birth, the newborn young are left completely alone but well concealed. Depending on the species, they may remain concealed anywhere from a week to a month. The young only emerge when their mother comes to feed them, usually two to four times during a 24-hour period. During this time the calf's scent gland remains inactive and the body wastes are retained until the calf is stimulated to void them by the mother's licking. During 'lying out' the mother remains on guard but stays some distance from the calf's hiding place. When the mother moves her calf to a new hiding place, the calf does not travel beside her but either runs ahead or alternately lags behind her. If the calf belongs to a species that lives in a herd, e.g. impala, when it eventually joins a herd with its mother, it will spend most of its time with other young, only seeking out its mother to feed or when the herd is on the move.

Beisa oryx and reticulated giraffe

Above: *A male reticulated giraffe in the Buffalo Springs National Reserve.*

Beisa oryx (Swahili: *choroa*)

Similar to the fringe-eared oryx (see page 36), the beisa oryx is greyer and paler and lacks the fringe on the ears. Otherwise their habits and social system are the same. Beisa oryx occur north of the Tana River and are quite common in the Samburu/Buffalo Springs Reserves.

Reticulated giraffe (Swahili: *twiga*)

Ancient peoples revered the giraffe and it is one of the most commonly depicted animals in prehistoric rock and cave paintings. Early written records describe the giraffe as 'magnificent in appearance, bizarre in form, unique in gait, colossal in height and inoffensive in character'. At one time it was even thought to be a cross between a camel and a leopard; this is why even today its scientific name is *Giraffa camelopardalis*. One of the earliest records of giraffe is when one was sent from Malindi to China as a gift in 1415.

Giraffes are the tallest animals in the world, 4.6–5.5m (15–18ft), and full-size bulls can reach up to 5.8m (19ft), outreaching all mammals other than elephants. The reticulated giraffe is the most handsome of all, with its chestnut-coloured body marked with a network of white lines, very different from the jagged blotches of the Masai giraffe.

Giraffe feed by browsing, using their long tongue (18in/45cm) to carefully select foliage, mostly from acacia trees. The narrow muzzle, an extremely flexible upper lip and the long tongue enable it to strip off branches or carefully select individual leaves from between long sharp thorns. Large male giraffe can reach at least 1m (3.3ft) higher than female giraffe and when feeding together the males feed high up while the females feed on vegetation below 2m

Kirk's and Gunther's dikdik

(6.6ft). When drinking, giraffe have either to spread or bend their legs in order to get down to water level. They have very elastic blood vessels and a series of valves that stop the blood rushing in and out of the head when raised or lowered. The giraffe's long neck surprisingly has the same number of vertebrae – seven – as man.

Even though they are often seen together in groups, giraffe form no lasting bonds and only associate with other giraffe on a casual basis. The group is constantly changing in make-up, because giraffe rarely form groups except when feeding on the same tree. Even so, giraffe are rarely out of sight of others due to their high vantage point. Young giraffe form into crèches with at least one adult female nearby.

Giraffes' two main horns differ from those of antelope and deer in that they are unattached to the skull at birth, slowly fusing to the skull at about four years old. During a male's lifetime bone accumulates at the base of the skull, above the eyes and on the nose, forming a massive heavy club which is used to gain dominance over younger bulls. Bulls sparring is called 'necking'; the males stand side by side and in turn swing their heads at each other's head or body. At times these blows can be very heavy but they usually separate before hurting each other too much.

Kirk's and Gunther's dikdik (Swahili: *digidigi* or *suguya*)

Dikdik are very small antelopes, only 35–40cm (14–16in) at the shoulder and weighing 4.5–5kg (10–12lb), hardly bigger than a hare. Gunther's dikdik occur in arid areas in Kenya, north of the Ewaso Ngiro River, while Kirk's prefer a moister savannah habitat. Both Kirk's and Gunther's occur together in the Samburu Reserve.

Male dikdik have small, straight horns which are absent in the females. At times the horns are difficult to see because of a shaggy crest of hair on the crown. Dikdik have large black eyes, which in the Kirk's are surrounded by a white ring, while in the Gunther's the white ring is incomplete. Below the eye is a very conspicuous black preorbital gland. These glands produce a dark, sticky secretion which dikdik deposit on grass stems and low twigs by inserting them into the gland. Dikdik have very large

Kirk's and Gunther's dikdik

Above: A female Kirk's dikdik. These small antelopes are very common and quite tame in the Buffalo Springs and Samburu national reserves.

noses which are almost like small trunks, being very flexible. The nose, though, is an adaptation for living in hot, dry climates; it has a blood-cooling function: blood is pumped into the nose where it is cooled before being returned to the body.

Dikdik live in pairs and are almost always accompanied by their latest offspring. It is said that they pair for life. They are very territorial; their territories are marked by the secretions from the preorbital gland on the face, foot glands and dung piles. Some of their dung piles (middens) are as large as 1m (3ft), and they have an unusual habit of dropping their dung on top of other animals' droppings, even those of elephants. This habit of trying to cover elephant dung with their own is behind an amusing African story. It is said that one day a dikdik tripped over some elephant dung, so from that day on, all dikdiks have kept piling their dung onto the elephants, in the hope of one day being able to trip up an elephant!

Both male and female help defend the territory, even preventing other females from entering it. The gestation period is just less than six months and a healthy female is able to conceive again in about 10 days' time. Unusually, a female dikdik is able to be pregnant and lactate at the same time. Dikdik are crepuscular (most active at twilight and just before dawn), feeding on the leaves of bushes, flowers, herbs and fruit; they do not need to drink as they get all the liquid they require from their food. When disturbed, they run in a series of zig-zag bounds; their alarm call is a shrill whistle, a 'zik-zik' cry, which is how they got their name.

Dwarf mongoose

The two species are difficult to tell apart: Gunther's dikdik do have a larger nose, and Kirk's have reddish legs while Gunther's are grey. Unfortunately, these two features cannot be completely relied upon, making their accurate identification very difficult.

Dwarf mongoose (Swahili: *nguchiro*)

As their name suggests, dwarf mongoose are the smallest of the six species of mongoose that occur in Kenya. Dwarf mongoose are short-tailed, stockily built and are a speckled reddish-brown in colour. They are highly gregarious, and live in groups of up to 20. They feed on a variety of insects, scorpions, lizards, snakes, birds and small rodents. When they find a snake, it is surrounded and each mongoose pounces at the victim, usually one at a time from different directions. The venom of spitting cobras does not appear to affect them. When hit, they back off, rub the venom off their fur and then go back into the attack.

Their social system is interesting; the group is led by a dominant matriarch who forms a dominant pair with her mate. This pair is the only one in the group that breed but the young are fed, groomed and looked after by any member of the group. The matriarch, being the pack leader, is the first to emerge from the den and is the first to set off foraging each morning. A group's territory averages 2.2km² (0.8 sq miles) and is defended vigorously. In the Masai Mara their territories often overlap those of the much larger banded mongoose; interestingly, it is the banded mongoose that give way in any confrontation between the two.

In Kenya's Tsavo National Park an interesting observation has been made. In this arid thornbush area, hornbills regularly forage with dwarf mongoose groups, hopping along the ground with them and eating the same prey. Interesting though, the hornbills give way to the mongoose, even juveniles, if both are competing for the same food item. Although the hornbills catch and eat other rodents which are often the same size as a baby mongoose, they never prey on them. The mongoose benefit from this association as the hornbills give warning calls if they spot any predators, in particular Eastern Pale Chanting Goshawks which are common in this area. When the group is accompanied by the hornbills they feel much more secure so post fewer lookouts.

Lizards

Vulturine Guineafowl

This large, spectacular, tall and long-tailed guineafowl occurs in dry bush country. The sexes are alike. They are very gregarious, usually occurring in large flocks, except when breeding. Their strident, almost metallic call is a feature of the areas where they live.

Somali Bee-eater

Somali Bee-eaters are small pale-looking bee-eaters found in the dry bush and semi-desert areas of Kenya. They are usually found in pairs, except when they have juveniles flying with them.

Agama lizards
(Swahili: *mjusi kafiri*)

Lizards are the most abundant and visible reptiles – no one visits Kenya without seeing a few lizards. Red-headed agama are usually seen sunning themselves on

Above: The more pointed head of this Nile monitor distinguishes it from a savannah monitor, which has a more blunt-shaped head.

rocks. The males have a vivid red-orange head (yellow in northern Kenya) and a bright blue body. Females and juveniles, by contrast, are dull brown with orange patches on their bodies. They live in colonies, with a dominant male who always basks in a prominent spot. When basking, the males bob up and down; this behaviour is sometimes not popular with Muslims, who believe the lizard is mocking their movement during their prayer. They feed mainly on insects.

Savannah monitor lizard (Swahili: *burukenge*)

Savannah monitors are most often seen sunning themselves on the top of a tall termite mound; when alarmed, they quickly disappear down into the mound. In the dry seasons they often aestivate (the summer version of hibernation), mostly hiding in a recess or hole. Occasionally, though, they are found aestivating lying along a tree branch completely in the open. If cornered they can be very aggressive, leaping at an aggressor and lashing out their tails from side to side, which can be quite accurate. They

The Samburu people

can also bite; although their teeth are not sharp, they nevertheless have been known to hang on like a bulldog. These large lizards can be up to 1.6m (5.2ft) in length. They are omnivorous and feed on a variety of food, including small mammals, birds and their eggs, other lizards, insects and carrion. Their enemies are Martial Eagles, and mongoose take their eggs.

The Samburu people

The Samburu are Maa-speaking people who live in the semi-desert of northern Kenya and, like the Maasai, are thought to have migrated southward to their present location several centuries ago. They are herders with cattle, sheep, goats and, more recently, camels. Milk and blood taken from the animals in their herds are their principal foods but they will slaughter a goat or a sheep on special occasions and also during periods of drought. They also collect roots and bark from certain trees to be made into soups. Unlike the Maasai, whose culture and language they share, they are much more tolerant towards other tribal groups.

Below: A young Samburu woman and child milking a goat. The Samburu people rely heavily on goats for their milk but they also utilize camel's milk.

LAKE NAKURU, LAKE BOGORIA, MOUNT LONGONOT AND HELL'S GATE

Lake Bogoria National Reserve
Nyahururu
Aberdare National Park
Nakuru
Njoro
Lake Nakuru National Park
Nyeri
Hell's Gate National Park
Mount Longonot National Park

This part of the Rift Valley is at times the home of millions of Lesser Flamingo and is a must-visit during any safari to Kenya. To view thousands of these birds against a backdrop of steaming hot springs and the sheer sides of the Rift Valley at Lake Bogoria is a sight never to be forgotten. Lake Bogoria is also the best spot in Kenya to see the magnificent greater kudu which, although sometimes difficult to spot, are quite common here. At Bogoria look out for the beautiful desert rose which when in flower is quite spectacular in this dry area.

Mount Longonot is a dormant volcano and it is possible to walk to the crater rim with a ranger escort. Near to Mount Longonot is Hell's Gate National Park which is popular with climbers who love to climb the sheer columnar basaltic cliffs which dominate this special national park. The cliffs are also a breeding place for Rüppell's Griffon Vultures.

Top Ten

Flamingos
Black rhino
Leopard
White rhino
Greater kudu
Great White Pelican
Rothchild's giraffe
Yellow-barked acacia forest
Black-and-white colobus monkeys
Crowned Eagle

Opposite, top to bottom: A breathtaking view of the dormant volcano, Mount Longonot, in the Rift Valley; a spectacular sight of flamingos at Lake Bogoria National Reserve; leopards are common at Lake Nakuru National Park.

Lake Nakuru National Park

Lake Nakuru National Park

Location: 170km (106 miles) from Nairobi.

Size: 188km² (73 sq miles).

Altitude: 1753–2073m (5350–6300ft).

Of interest: Gazetted in 1968, the park is open daily from dawn to dusk (06:00–19:00). Entry by smart card.

Accommodation:
Sarova Lion Hill:
www.sarovahotels.com
Lake Nakuru Lodge:
www.lakenakurulodge.com
Lake Elmenteita Lodge:
www.lakenakurulodge.com
Maili Saba (outside Nakuru Town on the rim of Menengai Crater):
www.mailisabacamp.com
Mbweha Camp (outside park):
www.mbwehacamp.com
Kigio Porini Camp (on the Naivasha – Nakuru Road):
sales@gamewatchers.co.ke

The Rift Valley's most famous lake, Nakuru, is known all over the world for its flamingos and has been recognized as being one of the natural wonders of the world. Roger Tory Peterson, the famous ornithologist, coined the headline phase 'The Greatest Bird Spectacle on Earth' on his first visit to Nakuru.

In 1961, the southern two-thirds of the lake was established by The Kenya Royal Parks as a sanctuary to protect the flamingos, and in 1967 Nakuru was declared a national park, the first one in Africa to be set aside for the preservation of bird life. The park's area was extended in 1969 to encompass the whole lake, and since then has been extended once more; it now covers an area of 188km² (73 sq miles). In 1986 the park was fenced with a solar-powered fence funded by Rhino Rescue Trust (UK) and in 1987 it gained status as an official rhino sanctuary. It is now harbouring a population of over 40 black and over 60 white rhino. In 1990 it was declared a Ramsar site, the first in East Africa, and in 2002 it was declared a World Heritage Site by UNESCO.

But the flamingos, of course, have always been the main attraction. At times there may be almost two million flamingos in residence, forming a stunningly beautiful deep-pink band around the edges of the lake shore. The lake is shallow and strongly alkaline (pH 10.4); this provides the ideal conditions for the growth of blue-green algae on which the flamingo feed.

During 1960 a small fish which is tolerant to alkaline water, *Tilapia grahami*, was initially introduced into the lake to control mosquito larvae; tilapia also feed on the blue-green algae. The tilapia have since multiplied both in number and in size, attracting large numbers of fish-eating birds such a pelicans, cormorants and herons.

Although over 400 species of bird have been recorded at Nakuru, they are not the only attraction the lake has to offer; over 50 species of mammal have been recorded here, and it is perhaps the best place in Kenya to see leopard and both rhino species. Some years ago a number of endangered Rothschild's giraffe were translocated here; they have multiplied and are now a common

Lake Nakuru National Park

sight. In fact their numbers have increased so well that several have been moved to other protected areas including Murchison Fall National Park in Uganda. Another of Nakuru's attractions are the troops of black-and-white colobus monkeys which can be seen in the Yellow-barked Acacia (*Acacia xanthophloea*) forest in the southern part of the sanctuary. This is also a good area to see the magnificent Crowned Eagle, Africa's most powerful, which preys upon the monkeys from time to time. Stretching along the eastern shore of the lake is a magnificent forest of Tree Euphorbias (*Euphorbia candelabrum*), unique in Kenya. It is, in fact, thought to be the largest euphorbia forest in Africa. Depending on local conditions the lake's size can vary between 5km² and 62km² (2–24 sq miles) in area.

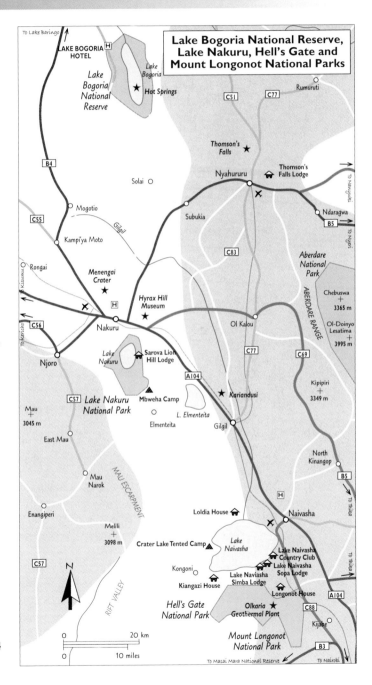

Lake Bogoria National Reserve, Lake Nakuru, Hell's Gate and Mount Longonot National Parks

Lake Nakuru National Park

Food for Thought

It is estimated that each Lesser Flamingo eats 184g (6.5oz) of spirulina a day. This means that a million Lesser Flamingo at Lake Nakuru consume 184 tons in a single day – about 66,300 tons a year! Add to this figure an estimated 2550 tons of fish, mostly consumed by White Pelicans, and it illustrates so well just how productive an alkaline lake such as Lake Nakuru can be.

Lake Baringo

Location: 280km (174 miles) north of Nairobi.
Size: ± 10km (6 miles) long, 6km (3.7 miles) wide.
Altitude: 975m (3200ft).
Of interest: Lake Baringo a well-known birding area (over 450 species recorded), surrounded by dry semi-desert country. Boat trips on the lake are popular – apart from seeing a variety of water birds, hippos and crocodiles are also commonly seen a very close quarters. One of the highlights of a boat trip is buying fish from a Njemp fisherman and then feeding them to the resident Fish Eagles.
Accommodation: see panel, page 95.

Flamingo (Swahili: *hero*)

The sight of as many as a million or more flamingos fringing a Rift Valley lake, like a river of flame, is one of the most breathtaking sights for many people on safari. The flamingo's name, which in Latin means 'flame', could not be more appropriate for these stunning birds.

Two types of flamingo occur in Kenya: the Greater Flamingo, which stands 1.5m (56in) tall, and the much smaller but much more numerous Lesser Flamingo, which is only 1m (40in) tall. Lesser Flamingo outnumber Greater by 200 to one. Lesser Flamingo eat blue-green algae, spirulina, which grows near the water's surface, while Greater Flamingo sift mud for tiny molluscs and crustaceans, and also spirulina, with their highly specialized bills. In ideal conditions it is thought that Lake Nakuru can produce 8 tons per acre of spirulina in a year. Both species feed with the bill immersed and their heads upside-down. Water is taken into the bill, which acts as a float, by a pumping action of the bird's tongue. The 'water' is filtered through dense filters, called lamellae, which line the inside of the flamingo's bill. Although flamingos find their food in the 'waters' of the alkaline lakes, they need clean fresh water to drink and bathe in. Flamingo congregate in large numbers at points where fresh water enters the lake; at times there can be long lines of flamingo queuing up for their time to drink and bathe. As flamingos spend so long in the caustic water it is very important that they bathe each day so as to keep their feathers in good condition for flight.

Flamingos are highly gregarious and nomadic, and fly in long skeins in a V-formation. Greater Flamingo occur in freshwater lakes and also in lagoons along the East African coast. Apart from being taller, the Greater species differ from the Lesser by being mostly white, with a contrasting bright red panel in the wing. The colours of the bills differ too. The Greater Flamingo has a pink bill with a black tip while the bill of the Lesser Flamingo is bright red with a black tip.

Flamingo are preyed upon by Marabou Storks and Fish Eagles. The storks, which look all the world like undertakers, slowly walk towards the feeding birds. At a certain distance the flamingos

Flamingo

quickly take flight and any ones slow to do so, such as sick birds, are quickly swooped upon by the storks. African Fish Eagles will also prey upon the flamingos, though they use a different technique. The Fish Eagles fly over the feeding flocks of flamingo, causing them to panic and take to the air. Again, if any of the flamingo are slow to take to the air, the Fish Eagle quickly swoops down on it, capturing and then dragging it to the shoreline, where it can be more easily eaten. Interestingly, at Lake Bogoria, Steppe Eagles, which are migrants from Eastern Europe and Russia, have learnt to pirate flamingos from the Fish Eagles. Steppe Eagles patiently wait until a Fish Eagle has caught a flamingo, then several of them will dive down onto the Fish Eagle forcing it to release its prize.

The words of the late Leslie Brown in his book *Mystery of the Flamingos* best describes them: 'In the early morning sunlight the pink of their plumage was exquisite, and their manifest excitement kept a forest of bright red legs and long pink necks always on the move. And they were more beautiful than I have ever imagined they could be.'

Rift Valley Lakes

Almost all of the lakes in the Rift Valley are soda or alkaline as they have no outlet. Their composition of trona or sodium carbonate is as a result of rivers, streams and springs having

Above: A group of Lesser Flamingo displaying along the shore of Lake Nakuru National Park.

Accommodation at Lake Baringo and Lake Bogoria

Lake Baringo Island Camp:
islandcamp@africaonline.co.ke
www.island-camp.com
Lake Baringo Club:
reservations@kenyahotelsltd.com
Budget Accommodation and camping site at Lake Baringo, Roberts Camp:
robertscamp@africaonline.co.ke
Lake Bogoria Hotel:
www.bogoriasparesort.com

96

Rift Valley Lakes

flowed into them for thousands of years through mineral-rich volcanic rocks and soils. This, combined with a hot climate, has concentrated the lake waters. However, lakes Baringo and Naivasha are surprisingly fresh, although they too appear to have no outlets. Lake Turkana, too, is only slightly alkaline. Some of the alkaline lakes do contain common salt which is produced in commercial quantities at Lake Magadi.

Rothschild's giraffe (Swahili: *twiga*)

Rothschild's giraffe occur in western Kenya (Ruma National Park) and differ from other giraffe mainly by the colour – rich chestnut patches separated by buffy lines – and having no marking below the knee. Male Rothschild's can have five horns, instead of the more usual two or four. Their social society is the same as that of other giraffes. The Rothschild's giraffe occurring in Lake Nakuru were moved there because of agricultural expansion in their original home, Soy, in western Kenya.

Below: A male mountain reedbuck keeps watch for any rivals and predators that might appear while his females feed.

Leopard (Swahili: *chui*)

An adult leopard weighs 30–80kg (65–180lb), making it much smaller than a lion. Its sandy-coloured coat is patterned with dark rosettes, not spots. Although leopards are mostly nocturnal, in areas where they are not harassed they can often be seen during the day. In fact, if hungry or if an opportunity of hunting arises, they will hunt during the day. Mostly they are found sleeping on a horizontal branch in a shady tree. Leopards mostly hunt by ambush, often leaping from a branch in a tree down onto their prey, usually seizing it by the throat. They usually take their prey high into a tree, well out of the way of spotted hyena or lions, sometimes still eating it days later when it has become rancid. This habit of storing food is very useful when a female has very young cubs as she need not spend time hunting. This means she can spend more time protecting her young from other predators, such as lion and hyena. This is very different from a cheetah mother, which has to leave its young, sometimes for long periods at a time, in

Mountain reedbuck

order to hunt. Occasionally, though, an agile young female lion will still manage to climb up and take the prey.

Leopards prey on a wide variety of animals – rodents, gazelle, warthog and even fish – and they also readily eat carrion. They are solitary animals, although their home ranges will often overlap. A male's home range will overlap those of several females. When a female comes into oestrus she is accompanied by a male for about a week before they return to their solitary ways. The gestation period is about 90 days, after which two to three cubs are born, usually in a cave, rock crevice or in thick bush. The cubs are born blind and their eyes open after about 10 days. The cubs remain hidden for about eight weeks and, although she will bring them meat at about six weeks, she will suckle them for about three months. Young leopards become independent at about 1½–2 years old but a female cub will often stay with its mother much longer, even when its mother has another litter.

Mountain reedbuck (Swahili: *tohe*)

Mountain reedbuck, smaller than the more common Chandler's reedbuck, inhabit steep rocky open slopes, grassy hills, escarpments and stony ridges. They are delicate and graceful, with a long, soft, greyish-fawn woolly coat which merges well with their surroundings. The horns, only on the male, typical of all reedbucks, are slender and curve upwards and forwards. Mountain reedbucks live in small herds of one dominant male with up to 10 females. They are very shy and alert and have a sharp whistle call when alarmed. Although they are mainly grazers they will browse on leaves and twigs in the dry season. Mountain reedbuck can be best seen in Lake Nakuru National Park and also along the escarpment on the edge of the Masai Mara National Park.

Long-tailed Widow Bird

Widow birds probably get their name from the fact that for part of the year during the breeding season, males grow black feathers over most of their body. Another explanation is that their long black tails are like a widow's train. The Long-tailed Widow Bird is no exception – in the breeding season it grows an extraordinary long floppy tail, while the rest of the body is black except for white-bordered red epaulettes. The male's tail is so long that it is

Hot Springs

Hot springs (*maji moto* in Swahili) and steam jets occur at a number of places in the Rift Valley. The best known ones are on the western shore of Lake Bogoria but there are also hot springs at Lake Magadi, Lake Baringo and at Kapedo, 50km (31 miles) north of Lake Baringo. Interestingly, the water supplying these hot springs at Kapedo is thought to come underground from Lake Baringo and this is the reason that Lake Baringo is a freshwater lake rather than alkaline. Steam jets are often used to supply drinking water. On the slopes of Mount Suswa local people place flat iron sheets over a steam jet and are rewarded by a steady drip of drinkable water. Kenya is now producing electricity from the steam in this area; one-fifth of Kenya's electricity supply is produced this way. Carbon dioxide gas seeping to the earth's surface is compressed into a liquid state and bottled; it is also made into dry ice for refrigeration.

Lake Bogoria National Reserve

Acacia No More!

At the 17th International Botanical Congress (IBC) held in Vienna, Austria, during July 2005, all 142 African acacia trees were controversially reclassified under one or the other of two newly constituted genera: _Vachellia_, comprising 73 species, and _Senegalia_, 69 species. The Yellow-barked Fever Tree now becomes _Senegalia xanthophloea_.

difficult for it to fly efficiently, especially in windy conditions. Long-tailed Widow Birds are usually found in marshy areas, where the male bird can be a spectacular sight, flying slowly and erratically, with its tail streaming out behind, looking like a large bustle. Males are polygamous and in the breeding season are very aggressive towards one another during the day but will roost with other males at night.

Yellow-barked acacia forest

Nineteenth-century explorers called this tree the 'fever tree' because it flourished in places of high ground water, which attracted mosquitoes. These beautiful flat-topped trees were believed by the early travellers and explorers to be the cause of malarial fever. The link between mosquitoes and malaria (literally meaning bad air) was not recognized until 1880.

Lake Bogoria National Reserve

Lake Bogoria (formerly known as Lake Hannington) and the surrounding area was established as a national reserve in 1983. Lying close to the base of the Ngendalel Escarpment, which rises 610m (2000ft) above the lake, Bogoria is scenically the most spectacular and dramatic of all the Rift Valley lakes. Long, narrow and deep, it is strongly alkaline and surrounded by dense, impenetrable thorn bush. Around the lake shore are a number of geysers and hot springs, which at dawn can sometimes form a thick mist. When one stands near one of the geysers and peers across the lake through the clouds of hot swirling steam to the towering wall of the escarpment, it is easy to imagine how the earth split apart to form the dramatic, chiselled sweep of the Rift Valley we know today.

There are times when Lake Bogoria is home to thousands of flamingos; to watch skeins of them flying along the lake towards the geysers and hot springs, where they drink and bathe, is a wondrous sight not easy to forget. John Walter Gregory, when he visited the lake during his explorations in 1893, called it 'the most beautiful sight in Africa'. Some years Lesser Flamingos build their cone-shaped mud nests at Bogoria and, though they occasionally lay eggs, strangely enough they have never been known to breed there. Bogoria is also home to a variety of

Rift Valley Volcanoes

mammals: common zebra, Grant's gazelle, impala, klipspringer, dikdik and the magnificent greater kudu, which is both prolific and tame here.

Desert rose (Swahili: *mdiga*)

Desert roses are found in Kenya's hot, arid regions and are thickset shrubs which in the dry season can look like miniature baobab trees. But when in flower they are transformed with striking pink flowers and they become a welcome sight in the drab-looking countryside where they occur. The sap is lethal: it's a potent toxin used to coat arrows.

Rift Valley Volcanoes

The whole length of the Rift Valley is studded with dormant volcanoes varying in size and shape. Some of them have the classic cone shape (Mount Longonot is a good example) while other, much older ones can be difficult to identify as volcanoes, because the original crater has been eroded away with time and only the hard central plug remains. Volcanoes situated in the Rift Valley are: North, Central and South Islands in Lake Turkana,

Lake Bogoria
National Reserve

Location: 80km (50 miles) north of Nakuru.

Size: 107km² (41 sq miles).

Altitude: 1000–1600m (3280–5250ft).

Of interest: Flamingos, hot springs, greater kudu.

Accommodation:
Lake Bogoria Hotel: tel: (051) 42733/40748.

Below: *The bubbling hot springs of Lake Bogoria bear witness that this part of the Rift Valley is still very active.*

Mount Longonot National Park

Mount Longonot National Park

Location: 80km (50 miles) from Nairobi.

Size: 52km² (20 sq miles).

Altitude: 1875–2776m (6152–9108ft).

Of interest: Gazetted in 1983.

Teleki's Volcano, Kakorinyo, Silali, Londiani, Menengai, Eburru, Longonot, Suswa, Olorgesailie and Shomboli.

Mount Longonot National Park

Mount Longonot is a majestic dormant volcano on the south side of Lake Naivasha. Although dormant, deep below the volcano there is water that is an incredible 304°C (579°F); this water is harnessed in the nearby Hell's Gate National Park at the Olkaria Geothermal Plant which supplies electricity to the national grid. There are a number of natural steam vents in the area which have been used by man for a very long time. The steam is condensed and collected as fresh water – very welcome in this dry area.

There is a well-defined track to the volcano's rim which visitors are allowed to walk, accompanied by an armed ranger. The view from the rim is staggering; the whole breadth of the Rift Valley can be seen, with the Mau Escarpment forming the western boundary and the Aberdare mountain range forming the eastern boundary with Lake Naivasha shimmering below. Joseph Thomson, the famous explorer, made the first recorded ascent in 1884. He wrote, 'The scene was of such an astounding character that I was completely fascinated and felt under an almost irresistible impulse madly to plunge into the fearful chasm'.

There are buffalo and colobus monkeys in the crater and it is sometimes possible to see the rare Lammergeier (Bearded Vulture) soaring by. Accommodation is available at Naivasha town.

Accommodation at Lake Naivasha

Loldia House:
www.governorscamp.com
Longonot House:
www.samawati.co.ke
Chui Lodge:
www.oserianwildlife.com
Lake Naivasha Sopa Resort:
www.sopalodges.com
Kiangazi House:
www.oserianwildlife.com
Crater Lake Tented Camp:
www.mericagrouphotels.com
Lake Naivasha Country Club:
reservations@kenyahotelsltd.com
Lake Naivasha Simba Lodge:
simbalodges@mitsuminet.com

Hell's Gate National Park

Hell's Gate, also known as Njorowa Gorge, is a deep gorge with impressive sheer columnar basaltic cliffs. The cliffs are of particular interest to birders and climbers. On the cliffs is a large breeding colony of Rüppell's Griffon Vultures as well as large colonies of Mottled and Nyanza Swifts. Verreaux's Eagles and Lammergeier can also occasionally be seen soaring along the cliff tops.

The gorge is an ancient outlet of Lake Naivasha and has a very prominent lone 25m (82ft) high volcanic plug called Fischer's Tower in its centre. This volcanic plug gets its name from the German naturalist and explorer, Gustav Fischer, who discovered the gorge in

Hell's Gate National Park

1883. There is a Maasai legend which relates how the tower came into being. One day the daughter of a senior member of the Maasai tribe left her home to get married. Tradition had it that she should not look back at her former home, but she turned around and was instantly turned into stone! On the 'tower' are families of rock hyrax and occasionally a pair of klipspringers. Other mammals occurring in the park are mountain reedbuck, eland, Masai giraffe, zebra, impala and both Thomson's and Grant 's gazelle.

Rock hyrax (Swahili: *pimbi*)

Rock hyraxes are small, furry animals weighing 2.5–5kg (5–9lb); they look a little like rabbits without the long ears. It is often said that the hyrax is the elephant's closest relative, but this is not true. The reason they were thought to be related to elephants is that their bone structure in the legs and feet is similar to that of elephants, the fact that males also have internal testes, and also the fact they have a long gestation period – seven to eight months. Rock hyraxes live in family groups of one male along with 20 or so females and their young. Each male defends his territory from other males. Rock hyrax have two or three young which at birth are remarkably developed – they can run about just one hour after birth. The young often form nursery groups. They are diurnal and feed on a grasses, herbage, leaves and fruit. They can survive without water but will drink when it is available. They use regular latrines, which form conspicuous white deposits on the face of rocks. In southern Africa these deposits are scraped off the rocks and sold for medical purposes; it is called 'Dassie Pee'.

Hell's Gate National Park

Location: 95km (59 miles) from Nairobi.
Size: 68km² (26.4 sq miles).
Altitude: 2777m (9111ft).
Of interest: Gazetted in 1984.

Left: A female hyrax, with her young, warming up in the early morning sun.

MOUNT KENYA NATIONAL PARK

M ount Kenya, at 5199m (17,058ft) the country's highest mountain, sits astride the equator; its higher slopes are permanently covered in ice and snow. The national park comprises the mountain above the 3200m (10,500ft) contour plus two salients astride the Naro Moru and Sirimon routes. The mountain is called 'Kirinyaga' by the Kikuyu, to whom it is sacred. The first European to climb Mount Kenya was Sir Halford Mackinder, in 1899. An old extinct volcano, it is made up of three peaks: Batian (the highest), Nelion and Lenana. Of these peaks, the original hard centre core is all that remains; the bulk of the volcano has been eroded away with time.

Top Ten

Scarlet-tufted Malachite Sunbird
Sykes' monkeys
Colobus monkeys
Suni
Crowned Eagle
Red-fronted Parrots
Black-fronted duiker
Giant heaths
Giant lobelias
Giant senecios

Opposite, top to bottom:
Looking over the alpine vegetation on the upper slopes of Mount Kenya down to the Rift Valley; a glacier below the peaks of Mount Kenya; a Sykes' monkey — these monkeys are quite common in the Kenya highlands.

Mount Kenya National Park

Location: 245km (152 miles) from Nairobi.

Size: 715km² (276 sq miles).

Altitude: 3353m (11,000ft) and above.

Of interest: The unusual alpine vegetation: giant heaths, lobelias and senecios.

Accommodation: *Mount Kenya Safari Club:* Kenya.reservations@fairmont.com *Naro Moru River Lodge:* alliance@africaonline.co.ke www.alliancehotels.com *Serena Mountain Lodge:* sales@serena.co.ke www.serenahotels.com *Warden's Cottage and Sirimon Bandas (both self-catering):* KWS Tourism Department tourism@kws.org

Mount Kenya National Park

Although conceived as a recreation area, the park has a good and varied population of wildlife, and is of geological and botanical interest. Elephant, buffalo and rhino are frequently seen as one slowly climbs upwards, and even when one is in the alpine zone just below the main peaks, there is wildlife in the form of giant rock hyraxes, begging for food from climbers if given the chance.

Scarlet-tufted Malachite Sunbird

Similar to the better known Malachite Sunbird but living at higher altitude, these birds have adapted to live on the special alpine plants that occur there. They feed on insects, flowering lobelias and senecios and nest in tussock grass or in the inflorescences of lobelias and senecios.

Climbing Mount Kenya

Mount Kenya is becoming increasingly popular with mountaineers from all over the world (Reinhold Messner, the first man to climb Mount Everest without oxygen, did much of his high-altitude and ice-climbing training on Mount Kenya). The main central peaks, Batian and Nelion, require ropes, ice axes and a degree of proficiency. Point Lenana by contrast is suitable for climbers with little experience. The four main routes to the peaks are: Naro Moru, the Sirimon and Timau tracks on the mountain's western slopes, and the Chogoria route on the eastern slopes. One can take a circular route or use a different track on the return

Right: Only experienced climbers should attempt to climb Mount Kenya.

Giant rock hyrax

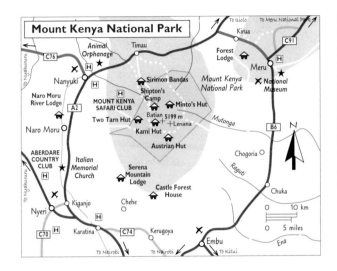

Hagenia trees

Hagenia are the dominant tree on the slopes of Mount Kenya, right up to the open moorlands. They are beautiful trees, with feathery leaves and, in season, hanging masses of tiny red flowers. They grow to a height of 20m (66ft) and are often festooned with 'old man's beard'. The wood is hard and dark red in colour, and is used in furniture-making.

journey (only for experienced climbers). Vegetation varies from dense montane forest and bamboo to gnarled hagenia trees draped with 'old man's beard'. Contact Naro Moru Lodge for details.

Giant rock hyrax (Swahili: *pimbi*)

The so-called giant hyrax are rock hyrax, *Procavia johnstoni mackinderi*, endemic to this area, that have adapted to a very cold climate. Their fur is much thicker than that of a normal rock hyrax, making them look much larger. They are quite common on the higher slopes of Mount Kenya where they are fed by climbers.

Sykes' monkey (Swahili: *kima*)

Sykes' monkeys are stoutly built, weighing up to 12kg (26lb), and live in forests. They are closely related to blue monkeys, but are larger and have thick, shaggy coats. They have a distinctive white throat and chest patch, and the bristly tufts of hair on their foreheads give them their alternate name 'diadem monkey'. Their walk is distinctive, moving their back legs in a gentle, trotting gait, and at the same time holding their long tails higher than the body. They live in groups with a dominant male and 10–12 females. Their main diet is forest fruits and insects and occasionally leaves. A good place to see them closely is at Serena Mountain Lodge on the slopes of Mount Kenya.

Afro-alpine vegetation

The height of the alpine heath zone differs from mountain to mountain depending on rainfall and the direction of the prevailing winds. Fascinating are the belts of giant heaths, hung with strands of 'old man's beard'. Giant lobelias, some 3m (10ft) tall, give way to giant groundsels which can grow to 9m (30ft). These high-altitude plants are specially adapted to withstand frost at night; the senecios, for example, close up tightly, only opening when the warm sun strikes them.

ABERDARE NATIONAL PARK

The Aberdare National Park is a wonderful area to visit. A 4WD vehicle is recommended as the roads can be tricky when wet. The scenery is quite spectacular with crystal-clear streams and a number of stunning waterfalls – 'The Guru' has a total fall of 457m (1500ft).

The moorland – with patches of giant heaths, which are so large that they can hide an elephant, and forest patches of hagenia, St John's wort and bamboo – is a wonderful area to explore. In the forest it is difficult to spot any wildlife but if the visitor drives slowly, with luck, leopard, suni and, perhaps, a shy rare bongo can be seen.

Experienced 4WD drivers can get permission from the warden to visit the Salient where Treetops and The Ark are situated. Although the forest is quite thick there is more wildlife here. In the open glades, look for giant forest hog, black rhino, bushbuck and the magnificent Crowned Eagle.

Top Ten

Leopard
Serval (melanistic)
Giant forest hog
Colobus monkey
Sykes' monkey
Suni
Crowned Eagle
Mountain Buzzard
Cinnamon-chested Bee-eater
Stunning waterfalls

Opposite, top to bottom:
A male Malachite Sunbird;
the interior of Treetops Lodge,
Kenya's most famous tree lodge;
a male bushbuck feeding in the
open – these normally shy
antelope are easily seen by
guests staying at Treetops
and the Ark.

Aberdare National Park

**Aberdare
National Park**

Location: 160km (62 miles)
north of Nairobi.

Size: 767km² (296 sq miles).

Altitude: 1829–3962m
(6000–13,000ft).

Of interest: Spectacular scenery
with stunning waterfalls and giant
alpine vegetation.

Accommodation:
The Ark: www.lonrhohotels.com
Aberdare Country Club:
www.lonrhohotels.com
Treetops:
treetops@aberdaresafarihotels.com
www.aberdaresafarihotels.com
Outspan Hotel:
www.aberdaresafarihotels.com

Now officially called Nyandarua (a Kikuyu name meaning 'a drying hide'), the Aberdares were given their original name by the explorer Joseph Thomson, who first saw the mountains in 1884 and named them after Lord Aberdare, then president of the Royal Geographical Society.

The park consists of the Aberdare mountain range running north to south and a thickly forested Salient which extends down the eastern slopes. On the eastern and western sides montane forest slowly gives way to bamboo and hagenia trees at the higher levels. In the north is Ol-Doinyo Satima, the highest peak at 3995m (13,000ft), and in the south the Kinangop. Between the two is an undulating moorland at an altitude of 3000m (9840ft), with scattered rocky outcrops, forest patches, highland bogs and streams. The moorland is covered in tussock grass, with areas of giant heaths so large they can easily hide an elephant, groundsels (senecios) and forest patches of hagenia, St John's wort and bamboo. A number of ice-cold crystal-clear streams, the Chania, Guru and Karura, cross the moorland, eventually cascading down the slopes in a series of waterfalls. The Guru at one point cascades more than 91m (300ft) down a cliff face and has a total fall of 457m (1500ft). The most accessible and widely photographed are the Chania Falls, sometimes known as Queen's Cave Waterfall after a visit by Queen Elizabeth II, who had lunch in a wooden pavilion overlooking the cascade. These streams hold both brown

Right: Giant forest hogs
eating mud containing essential
minerals at a salt lick in the
Aberdare National Park.

Aberdare National Park

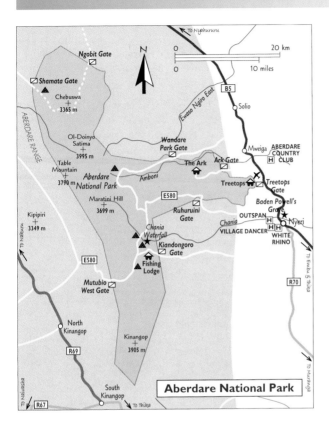

Aberdare National Park

and rainbow trout and there are two fishing camps on the
moorland to cater for keen anglers. The heavy rainfall in this
catchment area makes the tracks very difficult to navigate and
four-wheel-drive vehicles are essential. Animal life is prolific but
the thick forest habitat impedes game-viewing. Elephant, rhino,
buffalo, giant forest hog, bushbuck and both colobus and Sykes'
monkeys are common. Predators are well represented, among
them lion, leopard, hyena and serval (many of them melanistic).
Bird life, too, is abundant and varied: Cinnamon-chested Bee-eaters
nest in holes alongside the park's tracks, the Crowned Eagle –
Africa's most powerful – is common in the forest where it preys
on suni (a tiny antelope, smaller than a dikdik), while Mountain
Buzzards circle over the moorlands and Jackson's Francolins, only
found in Kenya, forage for food in the coarse tussock grass.

Aberdare National Park

The most convenient way to visit and experience the Aberdares is to spend a night at The Ark or Treetops, night game-viewing lodges located in the Salient. These two lodges are specifically designed to view the wildlife after dark. Both have flood-lit salt licks and water holes which can easily be seen from the lodges' rooms and balconies. It was at Treetops in November 1932 that Princess Elizabeth, who was on safari with her husband Prince Philip, became Queen Elizabeth II on the sudden death of her father, King George VI.

The whole of this wonderful national park is surrounded by small African *shambas* (farms) and large coffee estates. Because of the conflict between wildlife and farming, the entire perimeter of the national park is in the process of being surrounded by an electric fence, powered by water-driven generators. The enormous cost of this project is mostly being supported by local donations; an organization called Rhino Ark arranges fund-raising events such as motor sport and golf.

Below: The Ark stands looking over a water hole and salt lick, deep in the Aberdare forest.

Accommodation

Accommodation
The Ark
Guests booked into The Ark check in at the Aberdare Country Club where lunch is served. After lunch, they are taken by bus for a 30-minute drive through the Salient and on to The Ark. To enter The Ark guests walk along a raised wooden walkway with great views into the forest. On arrival, guests are briefed on such things as keeping as quiet as possible, times of meals and whether they need waking during the night if any exciting animal arrives at the water hole after they have retired for the night. The rooms are small but self-contained and look out on to the forest. At the end of the building there are two viewing platforms, one glassed in and one open. There is also a ground-level photographic hide where you can be almost at touching distance from the wildlife. After spending a night at The Ark, breakfast is served and guests are then taken back to the Aberdare Country Club.

Treetops
Guests visiting Treetops first of all stop off for lunch at the famous old colonial Outspan Hotel, in the small town of Nyeri. It is here that Lord Baden-Powell on his first visit said the following words: 'the wonderful views over the plains to the snow peaks of Mount Kenya …. The nearer to Nyeri, the nearer to bliss'. In the grounds of the Outspan Hotel there is a small cottage called 'Paxtu'; it is here that Lord Baden-Powell and his wife Lady Olave Baden-Powell spent the rest of their days. They are both buried in the churchyard at St Peter's Anglican Church, facing Mount Kenya. After lunch, guests are taken by bus to Treetops which is just inside the Salient. Treetops sits on stilts and is older and more rustic than The Ark. The majority of the rooms are tiny with no facilities; only the suites have en-suite facilities. There are shower and toilet facilities on the same floor as the rooms. After a night and breakfast at Treetops, guests are taken by bus back to Nyeri and the Outspan Hotel.

Animals
Bongo (Swahili: *bongo*)
The largest of the forest antelope, both males and females have spiralled lyre-shaped horns. They are bright chestnut red in colour, darkening with age, with 12 to 14 narrow white stripes on

Aberdare National Park

their shoulders, flanks and hindquarters. Running along the length of the spine is a black-and-white crest and between the eyes is a very conspicuous white chevron. There are two large white spots on each cheek. Bongos are extremely shy and are more usually found solitary, but occasionally they do form small groups of females and their young. Although mostly nocturnal they are occasionally active during the day. Bongos are browsers and are restricted to the higher elevations, usually occurring between 2100m and 3000m (6890–10,830ft) where suitable vegetation is available year-round. They range widely in the Aberdares, visiting the higher elevations during February and March before descending to the lower elevations during the wet seasons. At certain times of the year their main diet consists of bamboo which unfortunately periodically dies off after flowering. During the bamboo's second year of regrowth the plants become highly toxic; strangely, bongos do not seem to recognize this fact and many of them are poisoned. At one time they could regularly be seen at The Ark but, probably because of a combination of a bamboo die-off and the introduction of lions, they all but disappeared. Unfortunately, in unprotected areas bongos are very easily hunted by groups of hunters using dogs, which force the bongos to bay up, allowing the hunters to kill them easily with spears or guns. Happily bongos are now being seen more often, both at The Ark and on game drives in the area. At one place in the Salient a hide (blind) has been built to give visitors the chance of seeing this beautiful, elusive antelope.

Colobus monkeys (Swahili: *mbega mweupe*)

These beautiful black-and-white monkeys inhabit forests and are usually found feeding high in the trees, at 35–40m (115–131ft), where they can be surprisingly difficult to see. Colobus are very distinctive, with a black body, a contrasting white mantle and a long white bushy tail. Their faces appear to have white whiskers and a beard. The name colobus comes from a Greek word (*colobe*) meaning 'mutilated one' because they have no thumbs. Colobus monkeys spend almost all of their time in trees, rarely descending to the ground. They travel through the trees by jumping, sometimes as far as 15m (50ft), to get from one tree to another. Often they jump spectacularly outwards and downwards with their arms and legs outstretched until they reach another branch.

Colobus monkeys

Colobus live in family groups of 10–20 and they have very well-defined territories. Protection of their territories is mainly by bluff, aided by loud guttural roars. This calling is a distinctive sound heard by people camping in the areas where these monkeys live. Colobus feed almost entirely on young, tender leaves and have large stomachs which can hold the 2–3 kg (4.5–6.5 lb) of leaves they eat per day. Most of the feeding takes place in the early mornings and late afternoons; the rest of the day is spent grooming each other, paying particular attention to their long tails, and sleeping while their gut is breaking down the cellulose in the green leaves. Surprisingly, newborn colobus monkeys are pure white and it is not until they are one month old that they slowly change colour. At one time these monkeys were hunted for their beautiful fur which has resulted in their disappearance in some places outside protected areas. Their main natural threat comes from leopards and Crowned Eagles, and on a couple of occasions both leopard and a Crowned Eagle have been found feeding close to each other on parts of the same animal. Which made the kill, the leopard or the bird, is difficult to know. However, the loss of habitat is the most serious threat to their existence.

Above: A black-and-white colobus monkey resting in the forest on the slopes of the Aberdare National Park.

Aberdare National Park

Cape Chestnut

The Cape Chestnut (*Calodendrum capensis*) is one of the most beautiful flowering trees in the highlands of Kenya. It grows up to 20m (66ft) high and during the summer when it flowers, the forests are filled with beautiful rosy pink blossoms. Cape chestnuts are particularly common in the Aberdare National Park and along the Rift Valley escarpment near Nairobi.

Bushbuck (Swahili: *pongo* or *mbawala*)

Bushbuck are beautiful, shy, elusive, forest edge dwelling antelope and when seen are usually solitary, except when a female is with her latest offspring. Only male bushbucks have horns which are 25–55cm (10–22in) in length and grow straight back. The males are bright chestnut but slowly darken with age; some older ones look almost black. The females are similar to young males. Both sexes have distinctive white patches or spots on their ears, chin, tail, legs and neck, and a broad band at the base of the neck. Bushbucks are most active in the early mornings and late afternoons. They feed on a variety of foods, carefully selecting what they eat. They mainly feed on leguminous herbs, shrubs, fruits, pods, tubers, flowers and occasionally grass. If disturbed they often freeze and remain very still – their cryptic colouring is wonderful in helping them blend into their surroundings – or they bound away making a series of barks. Although not territorial, males will fight over any female in oestrus. After a gestation period of six months the female gives birth and then leaves the calf well hidden. The female only visits the calf to feed it during this 'lying out' period (see panel, page 83) which lasts about four months. Their principal predator is the leopard. Occasionally baboons catch and kill the calves, but even so it is quite common to see bushbuck feeding on fallen fruit that the baboons have dropped. Bushbuck are best seen at Treetops and The Ark.

Giant forest hog (Swahili: *nguruwe nyeusi*)

Giant forest hogs are large, ugly members of the pig family, covered in long black hair which becomes sparse with age. The males, which are 50kg (110lb) heavier than the female, weigh 140–275kg (309–606lb), and have large swollen preorbital glands which exude secretions that spread over the face. Both sexes have tusks, the male's tusks being thicker. In Kenya, giant forest hogs occur in highland forest with open areas of grassland. They feed on short green grass, fallen fruits and berries, and they dig out salty earth. Giant forest hogs live in family groups – a female with several generations of her young, 4–12 individuals. The males form small groups and older mature males live alone. While usually nocturnal, they have become diurnal in protected areas. They are best seen on drives in the Aberdare National Park, and at night at The Ark.

Sunbirds

Sunbirds, like the hummingbirds of the Americas, feed mostly on nectar taken from flowers. Of Africa's 70 species, 35 are resident in Kenya. It is possible to see 10 different sunbirds in a day at Naro Moru River Lodge. The birds are characterized by their thin, curved bills and the bright, colourful plumage of the males. When feeding on nectar, pollen from the flower brushes off onto the sunbird's forehead and, as the bird visits other flowers, is transferred from one blossom to another. This method of pollination is an extremely important exchange between bird and flower.

Golden-winged Sunbird

Male Golden-winged Sunbirds are unmistakable, with a long tail, bright yellow wing patches and a large strongly decurved bill. The bill is well adapted to feed on flowering crotalaria (lion's claw), leonotis plants and wild mint, which grow in the highlands where these birds live. Usually solitary, they are mostly seen along forest edges and in gardens. Breeding males have iridescent bronzy gold on head, neck and back, and black wings with yellow patches. The tail is long, with the central tail feathers elongated. The female, by contrast, lacks the long tail and is olive in colour. They are best seen in the Aberdare National Park.

Augur Buzzards

Once the most frequently seen bird of prey, unfortunately their numbers are now much reduced, probably due to modern farming practices. Augur Buzzards prefer open country such as moorlands, mountain forest glades and baobab country. They are usually seen perched on a prominent open branch of a tree or on a telephone pole. Their prey is almost entirely rodents, so they are a very valuable bird to humans. Unfortunately, they are often accused of raiding chicken pens, but all they are doing is looking for rats and mice that are attracted to the chicken food. In the highlands their main prey is giant mole rats.

Below: Augur Buzzards are characteristic birds of the Kenya highlands.

Aberdare National Park

Above: A stunning Hartlaub's Turaco. These turacos, although difficult to see, are common in the Aberdare National Park.

The reason there are fewer Augur Buzzards today is thought to be the practice of spraying agricultural crops with herbicides and pesticides. These chemicals kill any rodents in the area and these are then eaten by the buzzards.

Tree hyrax (Swahili: *perere*)

Tree hyrax are very similar to other hyrax but not as social. They are nocturnal animals and live in highland forest areas. Their loud call, heard after dark, is very unusual. It starts with a squeak, then rises to a squeal and finally ends with a child-like scream. They also have a harsh, rattling cry, like a heavy wooden ratchet being turned slowly, which is heard soon after dark; anyone who does not know them cannot believe that such a sound can come from such a small animal. They are hunted for their fur which is longer, thicker and softer than that of other hyrax. Tree hyrax feed on leaves and fruit, spending most of their time in trees.

Hartlaub's Turaco

Endemic to Africa, turacos are unusual birds. They have strong feet with semi-zygodactyl toes; the fourth is reversible and this allows them to run, climb and bound with amazing agility along branches. The feather colour of most other birds is produced by refraction of light from minute structures in the feathers but turacos have true pigmentation. The red pigment is known as turacin and the green pigment as turacoverdin.

The sexes are alike in colour, mostly green with brilliant crimson-red feathers in the wing, which are usually hidden from sight. However, once a turaco takes flight these crimson-red feathers are revealed, contrasting vividly with the green forest foliage. Turacos feed mostly on fruits, flowers, buds and insects. They are generally shy but their call, a series of loud raucous sounds, betrays their presence. Hartlaub's are resident in the highland forests of Kenya and are quite common in the Nairobi suburbs.

Jackson's chameleon (Swahili: *kinyonga*)

This is a large chameleon, the males being on average 38cm (15in) long. Males have three long horns which they use for fighting other males, while the females may have one or three short horns. The colour of the males is mostly green, while the females are mottled dull green or brown. Jackson's chameleons are found in highland forest, woodland and in cultivated gardens, where their diet consists mostly of insects. Females give birth to live young, usually from seven to 28 in number.

Mackinder's Eagle Owl

These owls are resident in alpine peaks and moorlands on Mount Kenya, the Aberdares and Mount Elgon; there are also small, isolated populations on cliffs, ravines and quarries at Lake Naivasha, Hell's Gate National Park and the area between Mount Kenya and the Aberdares. The best place to see one of these very special owls is along the Nyeri to Nyahururu road. Here local resident Paul Murithi will gladly show you one. Paul has persuaded the local farmers that the owl is beneficial to them because it feeds on rodents. Look out for a hand-painted sign on the roadside, 'Mackinder's Eagle Owl'. For more information, visit Paul's website at: www.owlspot.com

MASAI MARA AND RUMA

Big Cat Country, the Masai Mara National Reserve is lion country; a visitor would have to be very unlucky not to see lions even on a short stay here. Many of the male lions are black-maned and are truly magnificent animals. Cheetah are still quite common, and some of the cheetah are so tame and used to tourists that they often jump up onto the safari vehicle to look for their prey! Leopard, too, are quite common but much more difficult to spot. It is not at all unusual for visitors to see the Big Five (lion, leopard, black rhino, elephant and buffalo) on a morning's drive.

To visit the Masai Mara during the 'migration' is one of the natural wonders of the world. Over one million wildebeest on the move, accompanied by thousands of common zebra and gazelle, is a must to see for all wildlife enthusiasts. Bird-lovers too, will enjoy the Masai Mara which has recorded over 500 species, including 16 species of birds of prey. In the riverine forest bordering the Mara River, huge Black-and-white Casqued Hornbills can be seen and heard, while both Ross's and Schalow's Turaco are more difficult to see as they fly from tree to tree. The very unusual looking Double-toothed Barbet is also found in these forests. Added to all this are the wonderful Mara vistas which just beg to be photographed.

Top Ten

Black-maned lions
Cheetah
Leopard
Black rhino
Topi
Roan antelope (Ruma National Park)
Birds of prey – 16 species
Black-and-white Casqued Hornbill
Ross's Turaco
Stunning scenery

Opposite, top to bottom:
A lioness, feeding on its kill;
a Governors' Camp balloon
floating serenely over the
Masai Mara plains; two
male wildebeest fight in the
Masai Mara.

Masai Mara National Reserve

Location: 275km (171 miles) west of Nairobi.
Size: 1812km² (700 sq miles).
Altitude: 1650m (5414ft).
Of interest: Big Cat country; the famous wildebeest migration; wonderful scenery.
Accommodation: *see panels, pages 130 and 133*

Masai Mara National Reserve

Kenya's premier wildlife area, the famous Masai Mara National Reserve, is a six-hour drive west of Nairobi. The Masai Mara forms the northern extension of the Serengeti National Park in Tanzania. Wildlife moves freely between the Mara and the Serengeti and it is this freedom of movement which provides the greatest wildlife spectacle in Africa: the annual migration of wildebeest and other accompanying animals. The Mara, as it is generally known (a Maasai word meaning 'spotted' or 'dappled'), is a mosaic of rolling grassland dominated by red oat grass, small bush-covered hills and, along the Mara River and its tributaries flowing towards Lake Victoria, riverine bush and forest.

The reserve is well known for its black-maned lions and their prides, as well as its other abundant resident wildlife, and is one of the few places where it is possible to see the Big Five during a morning's game drive. However, it is perhaps more famous for its annual wildebeest migration – possibly the world's greatest wildlife spectacle (see page 20). The wildebeest population is now thought to number 1.4 million; accompanying them into the Mara may be as many as 550,000 gazelle, 200,000 zebra and 64,000 impala. Added to this are rhino, elephant, buffalo, warthog, giraffe, topi, kongoni (Coke's hartebeest), eland, leopard, cheetah, spotted hyena, and silver-backed and side-striped jackal. Other mammals that can be seen here are red-tailed and blue monkeys, banded mongoose, hippo, Defassa waterbuck, impala and bushbuck – 95 species in all. Many of the cheetah are so tame they seek shelter from the hot sun under the tourists' vehicles and several even climb onto the roofs to get a better view of any prospective prey.

For the bird enthusiast, almost 500 species have been recorded: among these are 16 species of eagle plus many hawks and falcons, six species of vulture, eight of stork, four of bustard (including the Kori Bustard, the world's heaviest flying bird), and nine species of sunbird. In the riverine forest it is possible to see both Ross's and Schalow's Turaco, Double-toothed Barbets and Narina Trogon. With this combination of wildlife and wonderful scenery, all under a great African sky, it is easy to see why the Masai Mara has become so popular among visitors.

Below: A majestic-looking male black-maned lion, posing for tourists, in the Masai Mara National Reserve.

Mara cats

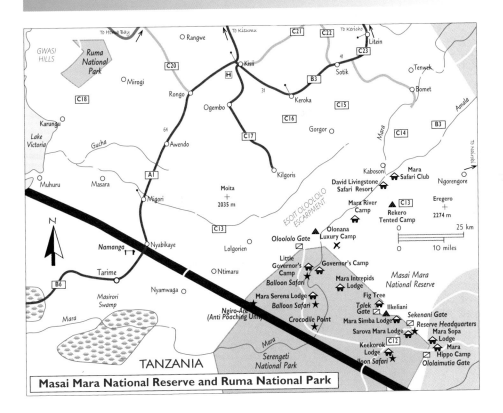

Masai Mara National Reserve and Ruma National Park

While staying in the Masai Mara it is possible to visit Lake Victoria. At dawn, a light aircraft takes tourists to spend a morning fishing or sightseeing on the lake, usually returning after lunch.

Mara cats

Lion (Swahili: *simba*)

Largest of the big cats, males can weigh up to 280kg (620lb), females 30–60 kg (66–132lb) less. Unlike most cats, lions live in a social system – an extended family called a pride. A pride is made up of a group of females, all related to each other (aunts, sisters), and their young, and one or two (occasionally three) males. Pride males are usually males of a similar age and quite often brothers. Generally the females hunt together as a team, but a lioness will occasionally hunt alone. Lions may hunt at any time but prefer night time when they are much more successful; even so, their success rate is only about

Masai Mara National Reserve

The world's first scheduled passenger service by balloon was launched in 1976 from Keekorok Lodge by Alan Root, the famous wildlife film-maker, and the late balloon pilot, Dudley Chignal. Now, at least six lodges offer hot-air balloon flights which, on landing, are followed by a glorious champagne breakfast cooked on site. Kenya is the only country in the world to offer such a high number of passenger balloon flights.

50%. Prey is knocked down and then killed with a bite to the throat or suffocated with the lion's mouth over that of its prey. Males do not often take part in the hunt and have gained a reputation of being lazy. This is not quite true; the male's role is mainly to patrol the territory to protect the pride from other prides and other males who would want to kill any young cubs. It is essential for the females to feel this protection. Of course, if the males are nearby when a kill is made they quickly arrive and take over the kill. When lion prides hunt large animals such as buffalo, very often the males will take part, their weight being very useful in bringing such an animal down. At any kill there is much fighting and squabbling, with the largest and strongest usually getting their fill first.

When prey is scarce the young and cubs often do not get enough to eat and starve. Lions are not always the noble hunters we think they are; it has been discovered that, certainly in the Serengeti, over 50% of the food is scavenged, mostly from hyenas that have originally made the kill. If there is more than one male in the pride, one will be dominant and it is he that will mate with any female in oestrus. Initially, mating takes place about once every 15–30 minutes and lasts for four to five days.

Gestation is on average 105 days and between two and six cubs are born. The cubs' eyes open when they are about a week old and they are helpless for the first few weeks. Newborn cubs weigh about 1.3kg (3lb) and are spotted. Very often one or more females in the pride will give birth approximately at the same time and the cubs are raised together, with any of the lactating females feeding the cubs. At about eight months the cubs are weaned and have lost most of their spots. At 18 months they are mature and it is around this time that young males will leave the pride, although occasionally the pride males will allow them to stay a little longer. These males will usually stay together, often joining up with other young males until they are strong enough to challenge for a pride. Pride males, usually 5–10 years old, are constantly challenged by nomadic males. Once a pride male has been driven out of his pride, he will mostly live off carrion until he dies.

Lions have long been killed in rituals of bravery; the Maasai are a good example of this tradition. At one time a Maasai warrior had

Cheetah

to kill a lion before he was accepted as a man and even now, although against the law, this is still practised. But it is not just in Africa that the lion has been idolized. In England the national football and cricket team have three lions as their emblem and the animal is used in many coats of arms and flags.

Cheetah (Swahili: *duma*)

The smallest of the Big Cats, on average 50kg (110lb), not only is a cheetah the fastest cat, with a top speed of 90–112kph (60–70mph), it is also the fastest animal. Although it is fast, it lacks stamina and cannot run at top speed for long distances; 300m (328yd) is about the limit. A cheetah's body is built for speed; it has a very flexible spine, long, slim, strong legs, a deep chest, a small head and a large heart. Its claws are only partially retractable, giving it extra grip in a chase, and a long slender tail gives it balance when making sharp turns. Although cheetah are similar in colour (tawny-yellow) to leopards, the cheetah has small round black spots on its body, not rosettes as a leopard has. Cheetah also have distinctive 'tear lines' that connect the inside corner of each eye to the mouth. Cheetahs are basically solitary animals, except when females have young or when a

Aloes

Around 60 species of aloe grow in East Africa; some species are eaten by elephants. The sap has been used by local people for many years for burns, insect bites and other injuries. Aloes are now grown commercially in the Rift Valley, for both cosmetic and medicinal use.

Below: *A mother cheetah with her cubs in the Masai Mara National Reserve.*

Masai Mara National Reserve

Lilies

Flame Lily (*Gloriosa superba*)
Flame lilies appear during the rains; they have spectacular red flowers which are often striped yellow or yellow-green. In Tsavo a variant is yellow with purple stripes. They are generally found in dryer areas.

Fireball Lily (*Scadoxus multiflorus*)
The beautiful red flowers appear before the leaves with the first rains. Fireball lilies are widespread in rocky places and open grassland.

male accompanies an oestrus female. Quite often though, young males (usually, but not necessarily, from the same litter) will stay together for a number of years. These coalitions of males are a formidable hunting team and can take on larger prey animals such as wildebeest and zebra. Cheetahs hunt during the day time, usually early mornings and late afternoons, but sometimes also on moonlight nights, and there are even records of them hunting in darkness. Although cheetahs live in the open plains and hunt by speed, they prefer taking cover until they can get sufficiently close to give chase. Then, with a burst of speed, they try to outrun their prey before reaching out with a paw and either knocking it over or hooking their sharp dew claw into it. The cheetah then quickly grabs its victim by the neck, slowly suffocating it. Cheetah often lose their prey to other predators such as hyena, lion, leopard and jackals, and even at times to large numbers of vultures. They eat their prey as quickly as possible, only stopping occasionally to check for danger. A cheetah's main prey is Thomson's and Grant's gazelle and their young, female impala and their young, and also young wildebeest. If a cheetah is disturbed and has to leave its prey it will not return to it; it also does not scavenge. This is a problem in some tourist areas where safari vehicles drive too close to feeding cheetah.

The cheetah's gestation period is 90–95 days after which two to five cubs (sometimes as many as eight) are born, usually but not always in a secluded place. The cubs are quite helpless and very vulnerable at this stage of their life, especially as the cheetah mother has to leave them on their own while she hunts. The cubs open their eyes at about 14–18 days and when they are six weeks old they are able to follow their mother. Before this time, the female cheetah moves her cubs several times to new dens. The cubs are suckled for about two to three months but are able to eat meat at about one month. Cheetah cubs at first have a mantle of long grey hair and their underparts are very dark, very unlike their mothers. At a distance, cheetah cubs at this age look very like the ratel (honey badger), which is reputed to be the fiercest of all African mammals. This is thought by some to be the reason for cheetah cubs looking so much like a ratel. Slowly they become lighter and the spots appear but cubs are sometimes 15 months or older before the grey mantle disappears. Although cheetahs purr, hiss and growl just like cats,

Serval cat and Nile crocodile

they have a chirping bird-like call to keep in contact with each other. Cheetahs are docile by nature and have been trained by man for a very long time, particularly in India. Akbar the Great was reputed to have kept as many as 1000 cheetahs. Their name comes from the Indian word for 'spotted one'.

Serval cat (Swahili: *mondo*)

This is a tall spotted cat, 56cm (22in), with long legs, very large oval-shaped ears and a short tail, weighing from 13.5kg (30–40lb). They are tan-coloured with black spots on the body, a black-and-white ringed tail and very distinctive white marks behind the ears. Occasionally, melanistic individuals occur, particularly in the highlands such as on the moorlands of the Aberdare National Park. Serval cats are shy, solitary and mainly nocturnal. Even if seen during the daytime, usually in the early morning or late afternoon, they can be very difficult to spot.

Their long legs are not adapted for fast running but to enable them to gain elevation when hunting in tall grass. They hunt with head high and ears cocked forward listening for their prey. Once prey is located they creep stealthily towards it, before leaping high through the grass and down onto their victim. Their prey includes young antelope, hares, rodents, snakes, lizards, birds, insects and even frogs. Servals often 'play' with their prey, tossing it high into the air several times before eating it. Where servals occur near man they are serious raiders on poultry, but, in turn, they are often preyed upon by hyena and larger cats, such as lion and leopard. Serval cats have large territories, sometimes as large as 8km² (3 sq miles). Females give birth after a gestation period of about 10 weeks, usually to two to four kittens.

Nile crocodile (Swahili: *mamba*)

Nile crocodiles can often exceed 5m (16ft) in length and weigh up to 1000kg (2204lb). They are fast swimmers and can even run fast on land; they also have excellent sight and hearing. Nile crocodiles are cold-blooded reptiles and depend on the external temperature to maintain their body heat. They can often be seen lying out on an exposed bank warming themselves in the sun. At times they open their jaws which is thought to help them regulate their temperature. When the sun is too hot, they go back into

The Candelabra Tree (*Euphorbia candelabrum*)

This cactus-like euphorbia can grow up to 15m (50ft). It has a short, thick trunk – up to 90cm (35in) in diameter – from which a number of spiny branches spread out, rather like a candelabra. Sometimes also known as a tree euphorbia, it is widespread in grasslands and thorn bush and often grows on termite mounds. It is most common in the Rift Valley, especially at Lake Nakuru, where there is a forest of them growing along the hillside on the eastern side of the lake. This forest of candelabra trees is one of the largest in Africa. Its branches are soft and brittle, and produce thick, sticky latex if broken. This latex is extremely toxic – a single drop in the eye can cause blindness – and it easily blisters the skin. The nomadic tribes of northeastern Kenya have a cure if they get this latex in their eyes: they quickly draw blood from a goat or sheep and pour it into the affected eye or eyes. The pain is quickly reduced and, apparently, the eyesight is not damaged! At times this euphorbia has flowers which are initially greenish-yellow but slowly turn pinkish, in groups of three to six. These flowers attract bees, but unfortunately any honey produced by the bees cannot be eaten, as it irritates and burns the mouth.

Masai Mara National Reserve

Right: A spotted hyena relaxing in the Masai Mara National Reserve.

the water to cool. Nile crocodiles are reputed to be able to stay submerged for up to one hour. Nile crocodiles have a varied diet ranging from insects when young to large mammals such as zebra, wildebeest and humans when adult. Prey is ambushed or stalked along the water's edge, with only the crocodile's eyes and nose visible above the water. Occasionally, if prey is a short distance from the river bank, they lunge completely out of the water to seize it and will sometimes use their tail to knock the victim into the water. Once in the water the prey, depending on its size, is thrashed around until a limb or part of the body is wrenched off. Also, when several crocodiles are feeding on a carcass at the same time, they will bite the carcass and then rotate several times until a piece of the victim is torn away. Crocodiles are unable to chew; they simply raise their heads and let the food fall down into the throat. Digestion is very slow and there have been incidents where a large crocodile has been shot and its victim has been recovered almost unmarked from inside the body. The female lays hard-shelled white eggs, usually 30–50, in a hole which she digs in a sand bank, usually near the water's edge. She covers the eggs after laying. Interestingly, the temperature of the buried eggs determines the sex of the young. When the young begin to break out of the eggs, the female crocodile digs into the hole and assists the young out of the eggs, even carrying them in her mouth down to the water where she can release them. Crocs have hardly changed since the days of the dinosaurs; a wonderful example can be seen at Koobi Fora on the shores of Lake Turkana.

Pyjama Lily

So called because their colour is supposed to be like traditional striped pyjamas, these are a member of the crinum family. These large, bulbous plants, whose heavy green leaves suddenly spring out of the ground during the rains, have long, tubular flowers coloured white with delicate pink stripes. They are widespread in Kenya.

Spotted hyena

Spotted hyena (Swahili: *fisi*)

The spotted hyena is both a skilful predator and an efficient scavenger. It weighs 40–86kg (88–189lb) and stands 70–91cm (28–36in) high at the shoulder. Unusually in the mammal world, the female is larger, on average 6kg (13lb), than the male and is dominant to the males. The sexes are very difficult to distinguish, apart from their size. For a long time hyenas were thought to be hermaphrodites, having both male and female sexual organs, and it was thought that they could change their sex at will! This was because the females' genitalia look very similar to those of the males. The reason for this, and the fact that the female is larger than the male, is thought to be so that the female can protect her young. It also gives her unimpeded access to any food. Hyenas live in clans of 30–80 adults. Within a clan of hyena there is a dominant female and it is this female that will often initiate a hunt. Interestingly her offspring usually eat better, grow faster and obtain higher ranking later in life. Spotted hyenas are social and communicate with calls and postures. When excited they hold their tails over their backs and when fighting the tail is held out straight, but when walking the tail is usually hanging down. If afraid, such as when they are chased away from a kill by lions, they slink away with the tail between the legs.

Clans consist of related individuals and they vigorously defend their territories from other clans. These territories are patrolled and marked with their anal glands and droppings. More often heard than seen, their long-distance call, a repetitive 'whoo-up', carries for up to 5km (3 miles); their well-known 'laugh' is a social appeasement call. A den, in which they raise their young, is usually situated in the centre of the territory and often on high ground, with good drainage and a good view of the surrounding area. The den will have several entrances that connect to underground tunnels; some dens have been used from time to time for many years. Two to four young are born (although rarely more than two survive) in a natal den, or a thicket or hollow near the den, after a gestation period of 90–110 days. Spotted hyena cubs are born with their eyes open but are initially partially blind. They are suckled for an unusually long time, 12–18 months, although they will start eating meat from kills made near the den from about five months old. This is thought to be because spotted hyena do

Gardenias

Gardenias are small trees and shrubs often eaten by elephants and giraffe which frequently crop them tightly, making them stunted and almost unrecognizable. Gardenias have heavily scented, creamy yellow flowers. In the Masai Mara they are often used by lions and cheetah to rest under during the hot hours.

Masai Mara National Reserve

Right: In the Masai Mara National Reserve, the icon of a male topi standing on a termite mound is a common sight.

not regurgitate food to their young and often have to hunt long distances from their den. In some areas, or at certain times of the year when their prey is scarce, they may be away from the den for up to a week at a time. Hyena hunt individually or in a group, mostly at night, their prey usually the more vulnerable animals such as young wildebeest rather than swifter, more abundant prey. They hunt by running down their prey and can run for long distances and as fast as 64kph (40mph).

Spotted hyena have massive, strong teeth and powerful jaws which can crack bones easily – the strength of a hyena's jaws has been measured at $800kg/cm^2$ (4520lb/sq in). Their digestive system is able to digest and break down bone, chitin and semi-poisonous compounds which are digested in only a few hours. The hyenas' massive teeth are able to cut through bones and skin, including that of elephants and rhino, leaving only the horns, hooves and some hair. It is this ability to utilize the remains of large animals more completely than any other carnivore that makes the hyena such a special animal. Other carnivores waste up to 40% of their kills. Interestingly, in the Ngorongoro Crater researchers found that it is more often the case that lions scavenge hyena kills than the other way round. This is almost certainly true in other wildlife areas too.

Unfortunately, hyena occasionally do kill human babies and small children and attacks on adults have been recorded. This may have arisen because some nomadic societies dispose of their dead and fatally ill by leaving the bodies outside the villages for the hyenas to eat. Although modern man mostly despises the hyena, in ancient Egypt they were domesticated, fattened and eaten.

Topi (Swahili: *nyamera*)

Topi are a familiar sentinel in the Masai Mara where their habit of standing on top of termite mounds is such a part of the scene. Males weigh on average 130kg (287lb) while the females are a little smaller, weighing about 108kg (238lb). They stand about 1–1.3m (3.25–4.25ft) at the shoulder. These antelopes have a short, glossy coat which is conspicuously coloured red-brown to purplish with distinctive blackish patches on the face, upper forelegs and on the hips and thighs. Their legs are yellowish, making them look as if they are wearing long stockings. Topi are almost exclusively grazers, living in open grasslands. They have a long, narrow muzzle and mobile lips which are adapted for selective feeding, eating only the tenderest green blades of grass. They are mostly gregarious, living in herds of 15–20, but at times congregate in much larger numbers. Usually a herd, which consists of one male and several females with their young, will hold a territory, defending it from other topi.

In the Masai Mara females form herds and move through the territories of different males. In these territories the male will have a small area of bare, trampled earth, very often an old termite mound on which he stands. This area is marked by dung piles and grass stems are marked by scent from his preorbital face glands. The male topi stands on these prominent mounds advertising his presence to all other male topi in the area. The males vigorously defend these territories from other males. Male topi fight by facing up to each other then going down on their knees to fight each other with their horns. Mating takes place

Nandi Flame Tree (*Spathodea campanulata*)

Called *kibobakasi* in Swahili, this tree is also known as the African tulip tree. It is native to western Kenya but has been planted throughout the country. When in flower this indigenous tree, standing 5–10m (16–33ft) in height, is spectacular. Its blooms are trumpet-shaped, about 12cm (4.7in) long, coloured orange/red, fringed with gold, and with a yellow-tinged throat. These flowers hold copious amounts of watery liquid.

Masai Mara National Reserve

within the territory and after a gestation period of eight months a single calf is born. Like other antelope the calves spend their first days 'lying out'. Reputed to be the fastest antelope with a bounding gait, they can outrun most predators.

Wildebeest or Western white-bearded gnu (Swahili: *nyumbu*)

The western white-bearded gnu is one of five distinct subspecies of wildebeest or gnu that occur in Africa but is the only one that still occurs in large migrating herds. Male wildebeest stand 125–145cm (50–58in) tall at the shoulder and weigh 120–270kg (265–600lb); the females are a little smaller, weighing about 45kg (100lb) less. Wildebeest are often called 'the clowns of the plains' because of their strange looks and, at times, their apparently strange behaviour. In fact, they are a very successful animal, exploiting the grasslands of the Serengeti/Mara fully to their benefit. They have an ability to locate unerringly areas of good grazing. Wildebeest are a keystone species and certainly not a clown; they have shaped and dominated their ecosystem for more than a million years. Wildebeest are pure grazers, inhabiting the open grassy plains, migrating only to follow the favourable conditions of grass.

Most wildebeest births take place in the early mornings, the actual birth taking about 1½ hours. The female wildebeest can delay delivery at any time if disturbed, at least until the calf's head and trunk emerge. Females lie on their side for delivery and the moment the calf is expelled the mother begins licking it. The newborn calf can stand within a few minutes and immediately seeks its mother's teat to suckle. Newborn calves are light tan in colour and are very active and able to run after about five minutes. As soon as the calf can run its mother quickly joins up with other females with calves to form a maternity herd. It may take from one to two days for the mother and calf to bond together and, should they become separated during this time, the calf easily becomes lost and tries to follow whatever is close by. It may be another wildebeest, another animal or a tourist vehicle or even, occasionally, a predator such as a lion. Any of these contacts can be disastrous to the calf. After two or three days the calves are able to keep up with the herds and their chances of survival are much improved. The main predators on the calves are hyena, but

Accommodation in Masai Mara

Mara Simba Lodge:
simbalodges@mitsuminet.com
Mara Siria Tented Camp:
www.mara-siria-camp.com
Mara Porini Camp (18km from the reserve; six tents on the banks of the Laetoli river: www.porini.com
Naibor Camp:
theartofadventures.com
Ol Seki: info@bush-and-beyond.com
Olonana Luxury Camp:
www.sanctuarylodges.com
Rekero Tented Camp:
info@bush-and-beyond.com
Richard's Camp:
www.chelipeacock.com
Saruni Camp (spa treatments inclusive): www.sarunicamp.com
Sarova Mara: www.sarovahotels.com
Sekenani Camp:
www.sekenanicamp.com
KWS Research Station (offers self-catering accommodation):
tourism@kws.org

Wildebeest

Left: Wildebeest crossing the Mara River during their famous migration.

lions, leopard and cheetah all take their toll. The calves are suckled for about four months but begin to eat grass at about 10 days old.

During the mating season, the large herds split up into smaller herds with five or six male wildebeest establishing territories within the herd. The males mark their territory with the scent glands on their face and between the two halves of their hooves. They also defecate and urinate at certain spots in this territory. The territorial males seem to go crazy, frantically leaping about, scent-marking nearby bushes and trees, and at the same time

Masai Mara National Reserve

grunting and snorting and foaming at the mouth. This may well be another reason why they are called 'clowns of the plains'. During this time territorial bulls have little time to eat or rest. The female wildebeest are only in oestrus for one day, so the males' behaviour is understandable – they have so little time to mate with the females.

Thomson's gazelle (Swahili: *swala tomi*)

Known to everyone as 'tommy' or 'tommies', Thomson's are much more numerous than the similar Grant's gazelle, although not as widely distributed. These small, graceful gazelles measure on average 62cm (24in) at the shoulder and weigh 17–29kg (37–64lb); the females are a little smaller. Males have strongly ridged horns while the females have short, pencil-thin horns, often malformed and broken, or none at all. Some scientists believe the females are slowly evolving and will eventually be hornless. This theory does seem a little odd though, because female Thomson's gazelle do try to protect their young by using their horns to fend off smaller predators such as silver-backed and side-striped jackal. Thomson's gazelle are well adapted to the open plains, where they are often seen with the similar-looking Grant's gazelle and other plains mammals, such as wildebeest and zebra. They migrate alongside wildebeest and zebra exploiting, like them, seasonally available grazing. They prefer short, green grass, so being among larger mammals is an advantage as the larger mammals either eat or trample down the long grass making the shoots of new grass more easily available. In the dry season they will browse on shrubs, legumes, seeds and even the fruits of the Sodom Apple (*solanum* sp.), which are poisonous to most other mammals. In burnt areas that have recently received rain Thomson's gazelle will sometimes congregate in large numbers to feed on the new shoots of grass that quickly appear.

They are dependent on water and sometimes are forced to walk up to 15km (9 miles) to find it. Otherwise they spread out over the plains, mostly in family groups of anything from five to 50. In the early mornings and late afternoons, the herds come much closer together; at this time the young often play, sprinting around the herd, with bouts of stotting or pronking (bouncing on stiff legs). Males take up territories and mark the boundaries with

Thomson's gazelle and Grant's gazelle

dung piles and tiny secretions from scent glands below each eye. These secretions are deposited on the end of growing grass stems by the male turning its head over to one side then carefully inserting the grass stem into his scent gland. These secretions can easily be seen, looking rather like a drop of tar at the end of the grass stem. When marking his territory with dung and urine, the male Thomson's gazelle makes an exaggerated display of defecating and urinating so any other males in sight can clearly see that a territory has been claimed. These territorial marks are made daily, especially if the herds are migrating and new territories must be established. These territories are vigorously defended from other males, with fights being common. The males face up to one another, clashing their horns, but there are frequent stops when both will begin to graze. At the end of a fight both males slowly move apart grazing as they go. Groups of females wander through these territories and the males attempt to keep them there for as long as possible. It is a common sight to see a male attempting to chase a female back into its territory. This is constantly happening so the size and composition of the groups of females are changing throughout the day.

Non-territorial males, usually immature or older males, form small groups of about 10, but occasionally up to 50 can group together. Very often older males keep to themselves which makes them much more vulnerable, so it is not surprising that it is these bachelor males which so often fall victim to cheetahs and leopards. The females breed twice a year after a gestation period of 5–6 months and although births can occur at almost any time of year, the peak time is after the rainy season. After birth, the young are left hidden in a clump of grass but if the grass is short the young are much more vulnerable as they can be more easily seen. The newborn young lie flat on the ground, stretched out absolutely still, and even though they are tawny brown in colour they can be amazingly difficult to see. The females visit their young to suckle them several times a day which is a very dangerous time for both the mother and young. Predation on the young is heavy, with cheetah, lion, leopard, hyena and jackal regularly hunting them. In certain areas baboons, particularly males, actively hunt for newborn 'tommies', and they are also eaten by eagles (such as Martial Eagles), pythons and caracal.

Accommodation in Masai Mara

Campi ya Tembo (book through Cheli and Peacock): tel 020 604054 or 603090/1.

Cottars 1920's: www.chelipeacock.com

David Livingstone Safari Resort: info@mugumo.com

Elephant Pepper Camp: www.chelipeacock.com

Fig Tree Camp: www.madahotels.com

Governors' Il Moran Camp, Governors' Camp, Little Governors' Camp and Governors' Private Camp: www.governorscamp.com

Ilkeliani: www.ilkeliani.com

Keekorok Lodge: www.discoverwilderness.com

Kitchwa Tembo Camp and Bateleur Camp: www.ccafrica.com

Leleshwa Camp: www.leleshwacamps.com

Mara Explorer Camp and Mara Intrepids Camp: www.heritage-eastafrica.com

Mara Safari Club: Kenya.reservations@fairmont.com

Mara Serena Safari Lodge: www.serenahotels.com

Mara Leisure Camp: www.maraleisurecamp.com

Mara Sopa Lodge: www.sopalodges.com

Grant's gazelle (Swahili: *swala granti*)

At first sight these are very similar to Thomson's gazelle, with which they are often found. They are similar in colour but Grant's gazelles are larger, standing 75–91cm (30–36in) high at the shoulder, longer legged and weigh 45–65kg (99–143lb). Females are a little smaller than males and both sexes have horns, although the males' horns are much longer, heavily ringed and thicker than those of the females. Some females have a dark stripe on the body making them look very similar to Thomson's gazelle, but both male and female Grant's gazelle have a white rump patch which extends over the tail, while Thomson's gazelle have a small white rump patch which does not extend over the tail. Grant's gazelle can tolerate very dry conditions, is more of a browser than a grazer and can live in waterless areas.

Grant's gazelle are gregarious, and herds consist of females and their young with a territorial male, or all-male herds. The female herds move through various males' territories while feeding, and each male will try to keep them and mate with any female that may be in oestrus. At the same time the male will often have to defend his territory from other males. Females give birth at almost any time of the year after a gestation period of about four months. Once the fawn can stand and has been cleaned by its mother, it takes its first feed, then moves away, followed by its mother, to a patch of grass

Below: A male Grant's gazelle checking to find out if a female is in oestrus.

Vultures

about 50m (55yd) away from its birthplace, where it will 'lie out' for 2–4 weeks . During this time the mother will stay close by but at times may be as far as 300m (328yd) away. The mother will visit the calf several times a day to suckle and to clean it. She approaches carefully to within about 50m (55yd) of the calf before calling it to her; they briefly touch noses before the calf quickly dives under its mother to suckle. Although the calf will begin to eat grass from about a month old, it is suckled for about six months.

Although Grant's gazelle have preorbital scent glands, they do not use them for marking as Thomson's gazelle do. A male marks its territory with dung piles and urine, doing this in an exaggerated posture so any other male in the area can see him. Grant's gazelle are preyed upon mostly by cheetah and leopard but their young are often killed by jackal. Pairs of jackal hunt for the concealed fawns during their 'lying out' period and although the mother can often chase away one jackal, she has little chance against two.

Ross's Turaco

Turacos are endemic to Africa. All are large, spectacular-looking birds, usually seen when trees are fruiting, or flying from tree to tree when the vivid red patches in their wings are so conspicuously seen. Ross's Turaco are dark, deep blue with an eye-catching bright yellow bill, a bright yellow patch around the eye, and a bright red crest on the top of their head. Turacos feed on fruiting trees and are mostly found in riverine forest. A good place to see them is at Governors' Camp, in the Masai Mara, where they have become used to people and are quite tame. Turacos are unusual in that their feathers have pigments (see page 117).

Vultures

Vultures are a familiar sight on safari, usually seen slowly circling high in the sky looking for any signs of dead mammals. Once a likely source is spotted, such as predators on a kill, or a mammal that has died of natural causes, they quickly spiral down and wait patiently for the predators to finish before they too can begin to feed. This descent is seen by other vultures which immediately descend to the same area. Often the first vultures to arrive are the Lappet-faced (sometimes called Nubian) Vulture, the largest of all the vultures. Lappet-faced Vultures have a large, powerful bill and are able if

The Difference Between Eagles and Vultures

While one is a mainly a predator and the other is a scavenger, the difference between them is mostly in their feet. Eagles and other birds of prey have large, strong feet and sharp talons with which they kill their prey. Vultures, because they do not kill their prey, have small, much weaker feet. The foot of a Martial Eagle is a good example of strong feet and long sharp talons for killing their prey.

Masai Mara National Reserve

Vultures in Trouble

Some time ago it was suddenly realized that the numbers of vultures on the Indian subcontinent had dropped dramatically. This was later found to be caused by the drug diclofenac used on cattle, which destroys the kidneys of any vulture feeding on dead cattle that had been treated by the drug. In Africa, too, vultures are either decreasing or, in some areas, particularly in West Africa, have disappeared completely. In West Africa it is thought that most have been killed by starving farmers during the ongoing Sahel drought. In some areas of Southern and East Africa, vulture parts such as eyes and their flesh and feathers are used by traditional medicine men for various reasons. Vultures are also inadvertently poisoned when they eat animals such as hyena that have been deliberately poisoned as pests in farming areas. It would be a very sad day if there were no more vultures in the African skies. The Red Data Status of East African vultures has recently been revised. The Egyptian Vulture is now regarded as endangered. Rüppell's Griffon Vultures and White-backed Vultures are now near threatened species. White-headed Vultures are now a vulnerable species.

necessary to tear open a carcass that has not been killed by mammal predators. The next to arrive are often the unusual White-headed Vultures which are a little smaller and are reputed to be able to kill small mammals such as hares and newborn gazelles. Like the Lappet-faced, the White-headed has a large, strong bill and is able to tear into any carcass. The next vultures to arrive will be White-backed and Rüppell's Griffon Vultures. Both of these vultures have long, virtually featherless necks, perfect for thrusting deep inside the carcass, and special tongues with backward-facing spines which help them feed inside the body. Rüppell's Griffon Vultures nest on cliffs while other vultures nest on the tops of trees, which means they often have to fly long distances from their nesting sites to areas where food may be available. For instance, there is a large colony of Rüppell's Griffon Vultures nesting on the Gol Mountains in the southern Serengeti National Park in Tanzania. When the famous wildebeest migration is in the Masai Mara National Reserve they may have to fly as far as 160km (100 miles) to find available food.

Two other vultures, one very common while the other has become inexplicably rare, can also be found near a carcass. The Hooded Vulture is quite common and is very often found scavenging in towns. Hooded Vultures have long, narrow beaks, they feed on scraps left by the other vultures and are also able to pick small pieces of meat off the bones and probe into broken bones for the marrow. The last vulture we may find on a carcass is the Egyptian Vulture. These distinctive-looking vultures with a narrow bill feed alongside the Hooded Vultures in a similar way. Egyptian Vultures are perhaps better known for their ability to use a tool. Egyptian Vultures break ostrich eggs by throwing a stone down on to them until they break. Another vulture found in Kenya is the Palm-nut Vulture; they are never found at kills with other vultures as they are solitary and feed on small animals and turtles, which they have almost certainly killed, and on the oil of palm nuts. In the Samburu/Buffalo Springs reserves, Palm-nut Vultures behave a little differently. They can often be seen feeding on bait put out for leopards by the Samburu Lodge and Samburu Serena Lodge, and on occasions they have also been seen feeding on the carcass of a mammal. Yet another vulture which has been recorded from time to time is the European Griffon Vulture. This rarely recorded vulture appears to be slowly becoming more common.

Snake Eagles

Left: A Rüppell's Griffon
Vulture about to land among
a group of Lappet-faced and
White-backed Vultures, feeding
on a carcass.

A group of vultures squabbling over a kill is an unbelievable scene. The sound, a variety of screaming, hissing, cackling and grunting, is amazing as they all fight for a piece of the carcass. The Lappet-faced Vultures, being the largest, try to dominate but are usually so outnumbered by White-backed and Rüppell's Griffon Vultures that even they have to back off for a while. But not for long – within a few moments the Lappet-faced will bound towards the kill, then dive onto the other vultures, driving them off for a short time.

Snake Eagles (Swahili: *mwewe*)

This is an interesting family of medium-sized eagles; all have distinctive bright yellow eyes and an owl-like head. They also have long, bare, heavily scaled legs which give them protection from snake bites. Five different species of Snake Eagle occur in Kenya, the commonest being the Black-breasted Snake Eagle and the Brown Snake Eagle which are usually found in open country, while the Western Banded and Southern Banded Snake Eagles are forest-edge birds. The fifth, the Short-toed Snake Eagle, is a rare visitor from Eastern Europe. All are usually solitary and easily seen as they often sit on exposed branches. Black-breasted Snake Eagles and, to a lesser extent, Brown Snake Eagles can often be seen hovering over the open plains. To see such a large bird hovering is quite a sight. When not hovering, they soar quite high in the sky looking out for their prey. When a snake is caught and the eagle needs to take it to its nest to feed its young, it does not carry it in its talons but partially swallows the snake, then flies away with the snake hanging from its bill. Both these species also

Masai Mara National Reserve

Right: Banded mongoose live in groups and are commonly seen in the Masai Mara National Reserve.

occasionally hunt from an exposed branch, dropping down onto their prey. The two Banded Snake Eagle species hunt from a low branch on the edge of the forest, dropping down onto any snake they spot below. When caught, the snake is carried in their talons to a convenient branch, where it is eaten. The Banded Snake Eagle has a distinctive strange mournful *ko-aaagh* call.

Banded mongoose (Swahili: *nguchiro*)

Banded mongoose are a common sight in the Masai Mara National Reserve. They are usually seen in a group, dashing away from a safari car. Occasionally, one or more members of the group will stop running and then stand upright on their hind legs, checking to see if the danger is real. At other times they can be seen in the early morning sunning themselves outside their den which is often in an old termite mound. They are gregarious, living in groups of about 15 to 20 individuals. The group is usually led by a dominant male and female and 3–4 other breeding pairs. The rest of the group is made up of non-breeding lower-ranking adults plus immature and young. Young males are thought to emigrate to other groups. Occasionally, a group can reach up to 40 individuals before splitting up. After a gestation period of two months, up to three or four young are born in the den. Any newborn young in the den are suckled by any lactating female of the group. They forage in a group, keeping contact with chirps and frequent twitters. If any become separated from the main group they become very upset, making a strident, shrilling alarm call. Groups can forage in an area up to 130ha (321 acres) which they defend from other banded mongoose groups. Banded mongoose mainly eat termites, insects and beetles and, only occasionally, snakes.

Warthog (Swahili: *ngiri*)

The warthog is a real character of the African savannah, perhaps nowadays better known as 'Pumba', the warthog character that starred in the film *The Lion King*. Warthogs weigh 90–113kg (200–250lb), the females being smaller, up to 22kg (50lb) lighter than the males. Although they are certainly not beautiful, they are fascinating animals. Warthogs are very distinctive, with a head that is large in comparison to its body, three pairs of warts on each side of its head, very often large sharp tusks, and a thin tail with a tuft of hair at its end. When running, warthogs characteristically hold their tails upright which always causes amusement among visitors. The tuft on the end of the tail is thought to act like a flag so any piglets running behind their mother can easily follow their mother and each other. Male warthogs fight either at a close distance or charge each other head-on; the warts act as pads protecting the eyes and face. Warthogs have four tusks; the ones in the upper jaw curve upwards and outwards, sometimes forming a semicircle around its snout. The tusks in the lower jaw fit against the upper ones and wear to a very sharp cutting edge which can cause serious cuts to

Left: A big male warthog poses for the photographer.

Ruma National Park

Accommodation at Lake Victoria

Lake Victoria Mfangano Camp:
info@governorscamp.com
www.governorscamp.com
Rusinga Island Lodge:
reservations@privatewilderness.com
Guests staying at Rusinga Island Lodge and Mfangano Lodge can arrange visits to Ruma National Park.

any predator trying to kill them. Warthogs usually trot, but can run surprisingly fast if chased by a predator. They are mainly grazers and are often seen kneeling as they graze short grass. They also dig up tubers and roots with their snout and tusks, a habit which causes much damage in agricultural areas. At times, particularly during droughts, warthogs will scavenge on carcasses left partially uneaten by predators. A large male warthog has been seen chasing a cheetah off its kill, a Thomson's gazelle, then beginning to eat the gazelle itself. Warthogs can survive without water for several months, can tolerate high temperatures and are able to conserve water inside the body. When water is available they will drink regularly and they enjoy mud wallows. Warthogs usually live in family groups of a female and her young; males only join a family group for mating. After a gestation period of about 175 days a litter of two to four young is born. Female warthogs have only four teats and each piglet will suckle exclusively from one teat – even if a piglet dies the remaining piglets will not suckle from the available teat. The young suckle for at least four months but start eating grass when about two months old. At night warthogs live in holes which they have excavated from existing smaller holes made by other animals. Warthogs reverse themselves into these holes so that they can defend themselves with their sharp tusks. Even so, they are often dug out of these holes by lions.

Ruma National Park

Location: 30km (19 miles) from Mbita.
Size: 120km² (46 sq miles).
Altitude: 1200–1600m (3937–5249ft).
Of interest: This park was previously called Lambwe Valley. Some of Kenya's last roan antelope can be found here, plus Jackson's hartebeest and Rothschild's giraffe. Ruma is also an important wintering area for the endangered Blue Swallow.

Ruma National Park

Originally established as a game reserve in 1966, mainly to protect a small herd of roan antelope, Ruma became a national park in 1983. It is only 30km (19 miles) from Homa Bay at Lake Victoria. The park is infested by tsetse fly, which has protected the area from encroachment by farmers. Recently though, the nearby research centre (International Centre for Insect Physiology and Ecology, or ICIPE) has devised new ways of controlling the tsetse and there is now pressure on the government to degazette the park. The park lies in the flat floor of Lambwe Valley bordered by the Kanyamaa Escarpment. The terrain is mainly rolling grassland, with tracts of woodland and thickets dominated by acacia and balanites species which tolerate the black cotton soil. Interesting wildlife found here includes Jackson's hartebeest, Rothschild's giraffe, topi, oribi and Bohor reedbuck. Bird life is good, with resident Bare-faced Go-away Birds, Mariqua Sunbirds and Silverbirds, and the area is an important

Roan Antelope and Oribi

wintering ground for the beautiful endangered Blue Swallow which breeds in South Africa. There is however no accommodation at Ruma; the nearest is at Mbita Point, 30km (19 miles) away.

Above: *A group of roan antelope feeding in the Ruma National Park.*

Roan Antelope (Swahili: *korongo*)

Roan are large and aggressive antelope, the males having horns which can grow to, on average, 70cm (27in) long. They are grazers and live in herds of up to 20; young males are tolerated within the herd until about two years old. Males live alongside the herd and actively exclude other males.

Oribi (Swahili: *taya*)

Oribi are small, graceful antelope with long legs and neck and a silky fawn/reddish-brown coat. Both sexes have a distinctive black spot below the ear and the male has thin horns, 8–19cm (3–7.5in) long. Males are territorial, mostly found with one mate, but occasionally a male will have two or more females resident within his territory. The oribi is a grazer which prefers grass that is shorter than itself but at the same time it needs cover nearby in which it can hide.

NATIONAL PARKS GUIDE

List of National Parks
Tsavo East NP
Tsavo West NP
Aberdares NP
Mt Kenya NP
Lake Nakuru NP
Amboseli NP
Nairobi NP
Meru NP
Kora NP
South Island NP (Lake Turkana)
Hells Gate NP
Mt Longonot NP
Ol Donyo Sabuk NP
Marsabit NP
Sibiloi NP: size 169km^2, altitude 2336–4321m
Saiwa Swamp NP
Ndere Island NP (Lake Victoria): size 4.2km^2, gazetted in 1986
Malka Mari NP
Chyulu Hills NP
Central Island NP (Lake Turkana)
Ruma NP
Arabuku Sokoke NP

List of National Reserves
Marsabit NR
South Turkana NR
Nasolot NR: size 92km^2, altitude 750–1500m
Nyambene NR
Shaba NR
Buffalo Springs NR
Bisanadi NR: size 606km^2, altitude 320–360m.
This reserve is adjacent to Meru National Park and is a
dispersal area for wildlife from Meru. There are currently
plans to upgrade this reserve.
Rahole NR
North Kitui NR
Lake Bogoria NR

Opposite, top to bottom:
A normally shy and nocturnal
side-striped jackal at dawn in
the Masai Mara National
Reserve; a male African (Cape)
buffalo accompanied by a cattle
egret; a herd of beisa oryx in
Buffalo Springs National
Reserve.

Kamnarok NR: size 88km²
Kerio Valley NR
Kakamega Forest National Reserve: size 45km²,
altitude 1520–1680m
Kakamega Forest is the easternmost remnant of the equatorial
rainforest that once stretched across Africa. Known as a bird-
watching destination, some 10–20% of reptiles, mammals and
birds found here occur nowhere else in Kenya.
Masai Mara NR
South Kitui NR
Mwea NR
Arawale NR
Boni NR
Dodori NR
Tana River Primate NR
Shimba Hills NR
Chepkitale NR
Losai NR
Mt Kenya NR
Laikipia NR

Below: A male Defassa
waterbuck feeding on the shore
of Lake Nakuru National
Park, with flamingoes in the
background.

Other Kenyan National Parks

National Sanctuaries
Maralal
Lake Simbi
Ondago Swamp
Kisumu Impala Park

Marine National Parks
Mombasa Marine NP
Watamu Marine NP
Kisite NP
Malindi Marine NP

Marine National Reserves
Malindi Marine NR
Watamu Marine NR
Mombasa Marine NR
Mpunguti NR
Kiunguti NR
Kiunga Marine NR

Biosphere Reserves
Kiunga Biosphere Reserve: size 250km^2
Mt Kulal Biosphere Reserve: size 7000km^2
Malindi/Watamu Biosphere Reserve: size 261km^2
Mt Kenya Biosphere Reserve: size 715km^2, includes Mt Kenya National Park at 580km^2

KWS Tourism Department
KWS Headquarters, tel: +254 (020) 501081 or 602345, e-mail: tourism@kws.org website: www.kws.org

Wildlife Conservation: Who owns What
Kenya has a total of 64 national parks, reserves and marine national parks and reserves; almost 10% of the country's land area is devoted to wildlife conservation. The national parks are owned by the government. A portion of the revenue earned by the parks and reserves is allocated to the local people living in the area; no human settlement is allowed. Local county councils own the national reserves; wildlife is protected and has precedence, some human habitation is permitted, and livestock may share the area at times. As for game sanctuaries and conservation areas, landowners can establish such areas to protect a particular animal or certain species of plant life. They are allowed to use the rest of their land for other purposes; a good example of this practice is Lewa Wildlife Conservancy.

National Parks Guide

Entry Requirements

Passport, valid from date of entry, is required by all. Nationals of the following countries do not need visas to travel to Kenya: Bahamas, Bangladesh, Barbados, Botswana, Brunei-Darussalam, Cyprus, Dominica, Ethiopia, Fiji Islands, Gambia, The, Ghana, Grenada, Jamaica, Kiribati, Lesotho, Malawi, Maldives, Mauritius, Namibia, Nauru, Papua New Guinea, Samoa, San Marino, Seychelles, Sierra Leone, Singapore, Solomon Islands, St Lucia, St Vincent & The Grenadines, Swaziland, Tanzania, Tonga, Turkey, Tuvalu, Uganda, Uruguay, Vanuatu, Zambia, Zimbabwe.

NB If you are NOT a citizen of any of the above countries and you wish to enter Kenya, you MUST OBTAIN A VISA IN ADVANCE, particularly if you are proceeding to Kenya from a country where there is a Kenyan Embassy, High Commission or Consulate to issue visa.

Applications from nationals of the following countries have to be referred to Nairobi for approval: Afghanistan, Armenia, Azerbaijan, Cameroon, Iran, Iraq, Lebanon, Libya, Mali,

Nigeria, North Korea, Pakistan, Senegal, Somalia, Tazikstan, Yemen, Stateless Persons. Persons falling under this category are advised to apply at least three months before the proposed date of travel to Kenya.

Health

Malaria

Malaria is very common in Sub-Saharan Africa. The predominant species is *Plasmodium falciparum*, the most dangerous of the four species of human malaria (the others are *P. Vivax, P. Ovale* and *P. Malariae*). Malaria causes an estimated 2.7 million deaths per year, with most of these deaths occurring in Africa. Ninety percent (90%) of the world's malaria cases occur in Africa. Chloroquine resistance is widespread in Africa. Now, malaria outbreaks are being reported in some locations of Africa that had been previously thought to be at elevations too high for malaria transmission, such as the highlands of Kenya. Some scientists hypothesize this is due to climatic change, while others think it is due to human migration. Also, malaria has resurged in certain locations of Africa that had previously had effective control programs, such as Madagascar, South

Africa, and Zanzibar. Malaria occurs in over 100 countries and territories. This use of prophylactic medication for malaria is very controversial, so visitors are recommended to contact their own doctor for advise.

Anthropod-borne Diseases

Anthropod-borne diseases such as malaria, plague, relapsing fever, Rift Valley fever, tick-bite fever, and typhus (mainly tick-borne) have been reported from most of this area. However, except for malaria (chloroquine resistant) in certain areas, they are not likely to be major health problems for the traveller. African sleeping sickness (trypanosomiasis) can occur. Various forms of filariasis, leishmaniasis, and tungiasis (skin penetration by larva of the female sand flea) may be found in some areas of Kenya.

Food- and Waterborne Diseases

Food- and waterborne diseases are common in some areas, particularly amebiasis and typhoid fever. Hepatitis A occurs in this area. Schistosomiasis is uncommon but does occur in some of Kenya's lakes.

Travel tips

Health Requirements

Recommended vaccinations for all travellers:
• Hepatitis A
• Typhoid
• Yellow fever (arriving from a yellow-fever-infected area)
• Polio
• Hepatitis B
• Rabies
• All travellers should be up to date on tetanus-diphtheria, measles-mumps-rubella, and varicella immunizations.

Health Precautions

• Drink only bottled water and drink it often to avoid dehydration.
• Avoid overexposure to the sun; most of Kenya's safari destinations are situated at high altitude (e.g. Lake Nakuru is at 6000ft, and Masai Mara at 5400ft), so it is very easy to get sunburnt.

Distances from Nairobi

Amboseli to Nairobi
  220km (137 miles)
Aberdares to Nairobi
  210km (130 miles)
Baringo to Nairobi
  280km (174 miles)
Masai Mara to Nairobi
  360km (224 miles)
Mombasa to Nairobi
  500km (311 miles)
Samburu to Nairobi
  355km (221 miles)

4WD Vehicle Hire

For safari-goers interested in hiring a 4WD vehicle, there are several options in Kenya:

Glen Mathews:
4WD self-drive Land Rovers equipped with winches and roof racks; e-mail: fourwdm@iconnect.co.ke

Roving Rovers: fully equipped (camping) Range Rovers; website: www.rovingrovers.com

Tough Tracks: for vehicle hire and also hiring camping equipment; website: www.toughtracks.com

Avis Rent-A-Car: www.avis.co.ke

Hertz: www.hertz.co.ke

Photography

Although Kenya is famous for being a land of photographic opportunities you must not attempt to photograph subjects such as the president, military installations, military personnel in uniform, police, prisons and prisoners. Remember that you should never photograph people without first asking their permission – Muslim women in traditional dress often dislike being photographed, and Maasai and Samburu warriors will expect to be recompensed for posing.

Film, both slide film and colour negative film, is widely available in Nairobi and Mombasa and in almost all safari lodges and camps. It is much cheaper in Nairobi – Expo Camera Centre on Mama Ngina Street is the cheapest. Camera batteries and video cassettes are not readily available from the camps and so it is advisable to stock up in Nairobi or Mombasa.

Still Photography

Two lenses are all that is needed for most wildlife photography, the exception being bird photography. A 28–85mm lens is adequate for photographing scenery and people, and a 100–300mm lens is ideal for taking general wildlife photographs. For bird photography, on the other hand, a lens of 400mm or more is required, especially for close-up photographs. There is often a temptation to make use of x2 extenders to double the magnification of the lens. Be warned that this makes focusing more difficult, and often the results are disappointing. However,

National Parks Guide

certain camera manufacturers such as Canon and Nikon produce a x1.4 extender, which, when used on a fixed 300mm or 400mm lens, can result in excellent photographs.

The really enthusiastic photographer is advised to bring two camera bodies. The second body is useful if you come across problems and it can also be loaded with a higher-speed film for those difficult shots early in the morning or late in the afternoon. For high-quality photography, slow film such as 50ASA, 64ASA or 100ASA should be used. It is also a good idea to fit a filter on the front of any lens to circumvent the dust problem. Use a small tripod that can rest on the vehicle's roof, or a beanbag to help keep the camera steady. To avoid missing any good shots, keep your camera ready to use. It is a good idea to have the camera switched on, resting on your knee and covered with a towel or kikoi (colourful African cloth).

Video Photography

Many visitors nowadays prefer using video cameras to still or movie cameras. The modern video camera is small and compact, making it very easy to use. Rather than moving it freely around, rest it on your vehicle's window-frame or roof, using a beanbag to keep it steady. (Bean bags are only supplied by one or two of the top safari companies so check before arrival). Better results will be obtained by letting the object move into or out of the viewfinder as opposed to following it as it moves. If possible watch a couple of wildlife films before you come on safari and note how the professionals do it.

Another tip is to keep the camera angle as low a possible, particularly if the subject is close, as it makes the subject much more impressive. The temptation is to stand and photograph out of the roof hatch and then have to look down on the subject which is not good photography.

Do not forget to use your video camera at night – it is amazing how well a video camera works in darkness, so if you are lucky and have a roaring lion outside your room or tent, have a go and film it (keep inside your room, of course); even if the picture is unclear, you will at least pick up the wonderful sounds.

Sound can either enhance or spoil the final result. Wind is perhaps the biggest problem, followed by chat from your safari companions. A special directional microphone fitted with a good wind cover is the answer to this problem.

Digital Photography

Many visitors now use digital cameras, ranging from the simple point-and-shoot variety to expensive ones with interchangeable lenses. In a digital camera, film has been replaced by a memory card (CF Compact Flash is the most common) which is available in various sizes from 128 MB to 8MB (in Nairobi 1MB is probably the largest available). Depending on the mode you select to capture your photographs in, RAW or JPEG, you can take as few as 20 images in RAW and nearly 300 images in small JPEG on a 128MB CF card. In large JPEG setting, 50 images are available on a 128MB CF card. Most photographers select Large JPEG but if you want to sell your photographs to a magazine its better to use the RAW setting. Many hotels, lodges and camps do not stock memory cards, so it is a very good idea to bring several spare cards on safari; even if they are available, they will be far more expensive than at home. Some digital photographers bring their laptop computers and download their photographs each day, but the extra weight may be a problem on small charter aircraft. Another solution is to carry a portable CD burner, and download your photographs onto CDs.

A problem for interchangeable lens cameras on safari is dust. When changing lenses some dust will enter the camera and will be attracted to the camera's charged sensors. This dust may be invisible to the eye, but will show on photographs. An air bulb can sometimes remove dust but in extreme cases the camera will have to be returned to the manufacturer for cleaning. DO NOT use an air can aerosol to clean a sensor because this can cause permanent damage. Because of this, many photographers never change a lens during a safari drive.

Binoculars

In order to benefit fully from your safari, it is essential that you have a pair of binoculars. Binoculars of the size 7X35 or 8X40, generally small in size and reasonably light in weight,

are strongly recommended. The first 7 or 8 represent the magnification and the second 35 or 40 refer to the diameter of the front lens in millimetres. Generally the larger diameter of the front lens, in relation to the size of the eye piece lens, the greater the amount of light gathered and, therefore, the brighter and clearer the image. Another easy way to check out the brightness of binoculars is to divide the second number (35) by the magnification (7) and the higher this number is (5) the brighter the binocular. It is a big temptation to buy larger magnification binoculars such as 10X40 or 10X50, but these tend to be heavy and cumbersome and are also difficult to hold steady. Fortunately with modern technology it is possible to purchase binoculars that have large magnification but have an image stabilizer system, unfortunately though, they are heavy and require batteries (dry cells) to run the stabilizing system.

Water

Water is a precious commodity in Africa. Please use water sparingly and do not waste it (e.g. when brushing teeth). Try to avoid unnecessary washing of hair, lengthy showers, etc.

Good Reading

Kingdon, Jonathan: The Kingdon Field Guide to African Mammals (1997). Natural World Academic Press.

Estes, Richard: The Behaviour Guide to African Mammals (1992). University of California Press.

Selected Animal and Bird Gallery

Elephant

White Rhino

Hippo

Buffalo

Blue Wildebeest

Burchell's Zebra

Banded Mongoose

Dwarf Mongoose

Reticulated Giraffe

Sykes' Monkey

Vervet Monkey

Lesser Bushbaby

Warthog

Yellow Baboon

Colobus Monkey

Rock Hyrax (Dassie)

Honey Badger (Ratel)

Nile Crocodile

Savannah Monitor Lizard

Agama Lizard

Animals

Lion

Cheetah

Caracal

Serval

Spotted Hyena

Leopard

Bongo

Hirola

Roan Antelope

Sable Antelope

Beisa Oryx

Oribi

Bushbuck

Eland

Reedbuck

Mountain Reedbuck

Impala

Kudu

Grant's Gazelle

Thomson's Gazelle

Sitatunga

Suni

Common Duiker

Klipspringer

Selected Animal and Bird Gallery

Crowned Eagle

Martial Eagle

Fish Eagle

Verreaux's Eagle

Southern Banded
Snake Eagle

Western Banded
Snake Eagle

Black-chested
Snake Eagle

Pygmy Falcon

Eastern Pale
Chanting Goshawk

Swallow-tailed Kite

Crested
Guineafowl

Vulturine
Guineafowl

Mottled Swift

Jackson's
Francolin

Black-tailed Godwit

Kori Bustard

Heuglin's Bustard

Green-headed
Oriole

Birds

Greater Flamingo

Lesser Flamingo

Pink-backed Pelican

White Pelican

Marabou Stork

Saddle-billed Stork

Pygmy Goose

African Finfoot

Long-toed Plover
(Lapwing)

Lesser Jacana

Black Heron

Bare-faced
Go-away Bird

Double-toothed
Barbet

Sokoke Pipit

Narina Trogon

Blue Swallow

Schalow's Turaco

Ross's Turaco

Fischer's Turaco

Hartlaub's Turaco

Selected Animal and Bird Gallery

Long-tailed
Widow Bird

Trumpeter Hornbill

Ground Hornbill

Silvery-cheeked
Hornbill

Red-billed
Hornbill

Madagascar
Bee-eater

Cinnamon-chested
Bee-eater

Northern
Carmine
Bee-eater

Black-and-white
Casqued Hornbill

Somali
Bee-eater

Red-fronted
Parrot

Scarlet-tufted
Malachite
Sunbird

Scarlet-chested
Sunbird

Orange-bellied
Parrot

White-starred
Forest Robin

Purple Gallinule

Black-breasted
Glossy Starling

Golden-breasted
Starling

Golden-winged
Sunbird

Birds

Rüppell's Griffon Vulture

Lappet-faced Vulture

Hooded Vulture

White-backed Vulture

Palm-nut Vulture

Mackinder's Eagle Owl

Lammergeier

Egyptian Vulture

Pel's Fishing Owl

Sokoke Scops Owl

Augur Buzzard

Grasshopper Buzzard

Lizard Buzzard

Klaas's Cuckoo

Lichtenstein's Sandgrouse

Two-banded Courser

Yellow-billed Oxpecker

Red-billed Oxpecker

Somali Courser

Rosy-patched Shrike

Check list

Top Mammals
- [ ] Ader's duiker
- [ ] Banded mongoose
- [ ] Beisa oryx
- [ ] Black rhino
- [ ] Black-fronted duiker
- [ ] Blue monkey
- [ ] Bohor reedbuck
- [ ] Bongo
- [ ] Buffalo
- [ ] Burchell's zebra
- [ ] Bushbaby
- [ ] Bushbuck
- [ ] Caracal
- [ ] Chandler's reedbuck
- [ ] Cheetah
- [ ] Coke's hartebeest (Kongoni)
- [ ] Colobus monkey
- [ ] Common duiker
- [ ] Common zebra
- [ ] Crested mangabey
- [ ] De Brazza monkey
- [ ] Defassa waterbuck
- [ ] Dwarf mongoose
- [ ] Eland
- [ ] Elephant
- [ ] Fringe-eared oryx
- [ ] Gerenuk
- [ ] Giant forest hog
- [ ] Giant forest squirrel
- [ ] Giant rock hyrax
- [ ] Golden-rumped elephant shrew
- [ ] Grant's gazelle
- [ ] Greater kudu
- [ ] Grevy's zebra
- [ ] Gunther's dikdik
- [ ] Hippo
- [ ] Hirola (Hunter's hartebeest)
- [ ] Impala
- [ ] Jackson's hartebeest
- [ ] Kirk's dikdik
- [ ] Klipspringer
- [ ] Leopard
- [ ] Lesser kudu
- [ ] Lion
- [ ] Masai giraffe
- [ ] Mountain reedbuck
- [ ] Olive baboon
- [ ] Oribi
- [ ] Ratel (honey badger)
- [ ] Red colobus
- [ ] Red duiker
- [ ] Red-tailed monkey
- [ ] Red-tailed squirrel
- [ ] Reedbuck
- [ ] Reticulated giraffe
- [ ] Roan antelope
- [ ] Rock hyrax
- [ ] Rothschild's giraffe
- [ ] Sable antelope
- [ ] Serval cat
- [ ] Side-striped jackal
- [ ] Silver-backed jackal
- [ ] Sitatunga
- [ ] Spotted hyena
- [ ] Spotted-necked otter
- [ ] Striped hyena
- [ ] Suni
- [ ] Sykes' monkey
- [ ] Tana River red colobus
- [ ] Thomson's gazelle
- [ ] Tiang
- [ ] Topi
- [ ] Tree hyrax
- [ ] Vervet monkey
- [ ] Warthog
- [ ] Waterbuck
- [ ] White rhino
- [ ] Wildebeest
- [ ] Yellow baboon

Top Reptiles
- [ ] Agama lizard
- [ ] Crocodile
- [ ] Jackson's chameleon
- [ ] Nile monitor lizard
- [ ] Savannah monitor lizard

Top Birds
- [ ] African Finfoot
- [ ] African Fish Eagle
- [ ] Arabian Bustard
- [ ] Augur Buzzard
- [ ] Bare-faced Go-away Bird
- [ ] Black Heron
- [ ] Black-and-white Casqued Hornbill
- [ ] Black-breasted Glossy Starling
- [ ] Black-breasted Snake Eagle
- [ ] Black-tailed Godwit
- [ ] Blue Swallow
- [ ] Brown Snake Eagle
- [ ] Carmine Bee-eater

Check list

☐☐ Cattle Egret
☐☐ Cinnamon-chested Bee-eater
☐☐ Crested Guineafowl
☐☐ Crested Lark
☐☐ Crowned Eagle
☐☐ Double-banded Courser
☐☐ Double-toothed Barbet
☐☐ Eastern Chanting Goshawk
☐☐ Eastern Pale Chanting Goshawk
☐☐ Egyptian Vulture
☐☐ European Griffon Vulture
☐☐ Fischer's Turaco
☐☐ Golden-breasted Starling
☐☐ Golden-winged Sunbird
☐☐ Grasshopper Buzzard
☐☐ Great White Pelican
☐☐ Greater Flamingo
☐☐ Green-headed Oriole
☐☐ Ground Hornbill
☐☐ Hartlaub's Turaco
☐☐ Heuglin's Bustard
☐☐ Hooded Vulture
☐☐ Jackson's Francolin

☐☐ Klaas's Cuckoo
☐☐ Kori Bustard
☐☐ Lammergeier (Bearded Vulture)
☐☐ Lappet-faced Vulture
☐☐ Lesser Flamingo
☐☐ Lesser Jacana
☐☐ Lichtenstein's Sandgrouse
☐☐ Lizard Buzzard
☐☐ Long-tailed Widow Bird
☐☐ Long-toed Plover (Lapwing)
☐☐ Mackinder's Eagle Owl
☐☐ Madagascar Bee-eater
☐☐ Malachite Sunbird
☐☐ Marabou Stork
☐☐ Mariqua Sunbird
☐☐ Martial Eagle
☐☐ Mottled Swift
☐☐ Mountain Buzzard
☐☐ Narina Trogon
☐☐ Northern Carmine Bee-eater
☐☐ Nyanza Swift
☐☐ Orange-bellied Parrot
☐☐ Ostrich
☐☐ Palm-nut Vulture
☐☐ Pel's Fishing Owl
☐☐ Peters' Finfoot
☐☐ Pink-backed Pelican
☐☐ Purple Gallinule
☐☐ Pygmy Duck
☐☐ Pygmy Falcon
☐☐ Pygmy Goose
☐☐ Red-billed Hornbill

☐☐ Red-billed Oxpecker
☐☐ Red-fronted Parrot
☐☐ Redshank
☐☐ Ross's Turaco
☐☐ Rosy-patched Shrike
☐☐ Rüppell's Griffon Vulture
☐☐ Saddle-billed Stork
☐☐ Scarlet-chested Sunbird
☐☐ Scarlet-tufted Malachite Sunbird
☐☐ Schalow's Turaco
☐☐ Short-crested Lark
☐☐ Short-toed Snake Eagle
☐☐ Silverbird
☐☐ Silvery-cheeked Hornbill
☐☐ Sokoke Pipit
☐☐ Sokoke Scops Owl
☐☐ Somali Bee-eater
☐☐ Somali Courser
☐☐ Somali Ostrich
☐☐ Southern Banded Snake Eagle
☐☐ Steppe Eagle
☐☐ Swallow-tailed Kite
☐☐ Trumpeter Hornbill
☐☐ Verreaux's Eagle
☐☐ Vulturine Guineafowl
☐☐ Wahlberg's Eagle
☐☐ Western Banded Snake Eagle
   White Pelican
☐☐ White-backed Vulture
☐☐ White-starred Forest Robin
☐☐ Yellow-billed Oxpecker

Index

Index

Imprint Page

First edition published in 2007
by New Holland Publishers (UK) Ltd
London • Cape Town • Sydney • Auckland
10 9 8 7 6 5 4 3 2 1
website: www.newhollandpublishers.com

Garfield House, 86 Edgware Road
London W2 2EA
United Kingdom

80 McKenzie Street
Cape Town 8001
South Africa

218 Lake Road
Northcote, Auckland
New Zealand

14 Aquatic Drive
Frenchs Forest NSW 2086
Australia

Distributed in the USA by
The Globe Pequot Press, Connecticut

Keep us Current
Information in travel guides is apt to change, which is
why we regularly update our guides. We'd be grateful
to receive feedback if you've noted something we
should include in our updates. If you have new information, please share it with us by writing to the
Publishing Manager, Globetrotter, at the office nearest
to you (addresses on this page). The most significant
contribution to each new edition will receive a free
copy of the updated guide.

Publishing Manager: Thea Grobbelaar
DTP Cartographic Manager: Genené Hart
Editor: Thea Grobbelaar
Design and DTP: Nicole Bannister
Cartographer: Nicole Bannister
Picture Researcher: Shavonne Govender
Illustrators: Steven Felmore (birds), Michael Thayer
(reptiles), Penny Meakin, Michael Thayer and Steven
Felmore (mammals)

Reproduction by Resolution, Cape Town
Printed and bound by Star Standard Industries (Pte)
Ltd, Singapore

Acknowledgments: The authors wish to thank
Patrick Reynolds for his valuable help. Also Lis Farrell
and Jeremy Watkins-Pitchford without whom we
could not have
completed this project.

Photographic credits:
Africa Imagery: pages 12, 15, 24 (centre), 50 (top),
56 (centre and bottom), 89, 90 (bottom), 96, 102
(bottom), 106 (top and centre), 110, 113, 118 (top),
126; **Darryl & Sharna Balfour/IOA:** front cover,
title page, pages 6 (bottom), 21 (left and right), 24
(bottom), 40 (top and bottom), 50 (centre and
bottom), 52, 63, 86, 90 (centre), 99, 142 (bottom);
Andrew Bannister/IOA: back cover (top and
bottom), contents page, pages 26, 35, 40 (centre), 42,
46, 69, 72 (top), 102 (top), 139, 142 (centre); **Nigel
Dennis/IOA:** pages 61, 62; **Martin Harvey/IOA:**
half title page, pages 24 (top), 29, 30, 118 (centre and
bottom), 128, 134, 137; **Ian Michler/IOA:** pages 18,
56 (top); **Peter Pickford/IOA:** pages 115, 138;
Ariadne van Zandbergen/IOA: pages 71, 88, 106
(bottom), 131; **Chanan Weiss/IOA:** pages 6 (centre),
102 (centre), 104; **Dave Richards:** back cover (centre),
pages 6 (top), 9, 23, 37, 38, 47, 49, 64 (top, centre and
bottom), 72 (centre and bottom), 81, 84, 90 (top), 95,
101, 108, 116, 120, 123, 141, 142 (top), 144.
[IOA = Images of Africa.]

Cover: *Elephants in Amboseli, with Kilimanjaro in the
background (front); Mara River, cheetah in Masai Mara,
African Spoonbills (back, top to bottom).*
Half title page: *Vultures in an acacia tree, Masai Mara.*
Title page: *Elephants in Amboseli.*